CONTENTS

INTRODUCTION

YES, THIS GUY

"I WAS SO LAME IN HIGH SCHOOL. I DIDN'T HAVE ANY FRIENDS."

—Pete Davidson, Sundance Film Festival interview, E! Online, January 28, 2019

Most of us might not remember much from high school. But a few things stick. 1492. Pi. Periodic table. Smoot-Hawley Tariff Act. We may not really know what those things are. But we remember that they are definitely things. Things that we are supposed to know.

But what does that have to do with Pete Davidson, you ask? Patience, grasshopper.

The other thing we remember from back then is pecking orders. High school was the time when we were subject to the inscrutable and fairly ruthless manner in which the classmates whose opinion mattered determined who was dateable and who was not. Whether we liked it or not, we all had a fairly good idea of where we stood in that order.

If the old saying is right, and Hollywood is just high school with money, it seems somewhat clear where Pete Davidson would fit in. He is a stand-up comic and self-identified un-athletic nerd covered in unusual tattoos, often giving off a vibe that borders on the dorky, frequently a bit off due to various substances, and unlikely to be immediately popular enough to be class clown. In high school, this would probably lead to him being slotted into some lower-ranking or off-to-one-side "Outsider" or "Other, Miscellaneous" category.

Yet somehow, in the past few years, Pete, who should be an "Other, Miscellaneous" guy according to all rules of social order, has dated a slew of gorgeous women—a Grammy-winning pop star, models, actresses, mega-influencers—identified by many as out of his league. Pete does not make sense in the celebrity pecking order. Not a bit. But yet here we are in awe of a man who has something to teach the rest of us about attractiveness, romance, and dating. In fact, he appears to have created an entirely new category of date-ability that few of us knew existed: ugly hot.

Pete frequently talks about the fluctuating state of his mental health and his stints in rehab. For lengthy stretches during his adulthood, he lived in his mother's basement. He has tattoos of the owl from the old Tootsie Pop commercials and Winnie the Pooh,[1] not to mention inky scrawls referring to any number of ex-girlfriends.

So, what is Pete doing that allows him to level up? And what can people do to emulate his success, but perhaps with fewer tattoos?

This book is your chance to find out.

---

1. Permanently. On his body.

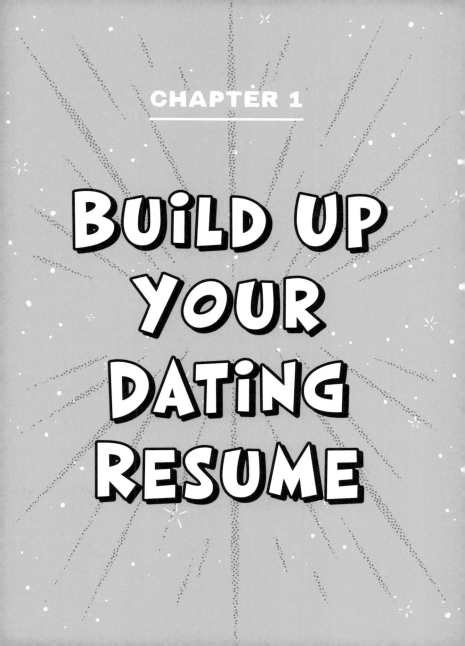

CHAPTER 1

BUILD UP YOUR DATING RESUME

"ONE OF LIFE'S **GREAT SECRETS**: WOMEN DON'T LOOK FOR **HANDSOME MEN,** THEY LOOK FOR MEN WITH **BEAUTIFUL WOMEN**."

—*The Book of Laughter and Forgetting*, Milan Kundera, 1980

I t is a truth universally acknowledged that once a guy has gone out with a woman of higher status than himself, his stock inevitably rises.

Everybody has known a version of this guy at some point in their lives. Normal-seeming, maybe a little shy, not particularly striking, maybe a little funny at times (both funny ha-ha and funny weird). Not undateable by any means. But also not known for always having a girlfriend. But then one day, this guy shows up with a woman who by general consensus is clearly out of his league. This can cause surprise ("What's she doing with him?") and even elicit consternation from some.[2]

At the same time, after a man is romantically attached to one woman perceived to be of higher status, that can

---

2. Colloquially known as the "Is She Really Going Out with Him?" factor, per Joe Jackson ("'Cause if my eyes don't deceive me / There's something going wrong around here").

build a certain kind of momentum. Once a man has essentially proven to others that he has the potential to attract a woman who it is assumed would normally not bother answering his texts, he moves up a rung in the highly complex and little understood matrix of relationship status. He is dating up.

The question of whether or not she believes she is dating down by going out with him does not appear to haunt somebody with Pete's refusal to think too much of himself (he did refer to himself and other Staten Islanders as "garbage people"). Where does this lack of ego come from? Maybe it's innate humility, blue-collar modesty, or anxiety. We may never know. Whatever magical combination of qualities paved the way for it, dating up is one particular maneuver that Pete Davidson executes with skill. His success appears to have bred success. People have noticed and women, in particular, have paid attention.

It is hard to overestimate the importance of who a man is spotted with. But not all of the attention that Pete gets can be attributed to people fascinated by his celebrity dates. Some, or even possibly a lot of it, is because of Pete himself.

When Pete was starting his career in 2013, he would probably not have ranked very high on a celebrity desirability meter. At the time, he was just one of the guys on MTV2's not especially buzz-worthy show *Guy Code*. For a time, he and his co-star comedian Carly Aquilino went

(CONTINUED ON PAGE 12)

9

THE SCIENCE

Mate choice copying is a neurobiologically influenced kind of social learning through which different species weed out mates by assessing their desirability based on who else they have been linked to. Scientific research conducted by people smart enough to use the term "game theory" and know what it means[3] discovered this same behavior in people. In a 2018 study, women were more likely to rate a man as desirable when he was shown with another woman (Street et al. 2018). Additionally, a different study revealed that women shown pictures of men with women described as their girlfriends were rated as more desirable if their girlfriend was considered attractive (Vakirtzis and Roberts 2010).

---

3. No, Monopoly is not involved. Disappointing, yes?

ᴏꜰ PETE

One hypothesis is that women engage in a kind of crowd-sourcing: Rather than date one unacceptable guy after another, they might find it more efficient to select from the men already chosen by other beautiful women (who, given their superior looks, would not dream of settling for someone unacceptable).

This explains why some men who are not Pete will hire "wing women" to accompany them on their nights out; they know that being seen hanging out with a good-looking woman will increase their status. The risk they take is that potential dates might think he is already taken.

out, sort of. As far as gossip attention goes, this relationship did not garner much at all since neither of them was particularly well-known (Pete didn't join *Saturday Night Live* until the following year). However, for Pete, just having it out there that the self-admittedly socially awkward young guy who was extremely unpopular in high school had a girlfriend (even if it was casual) was a start. Their having what

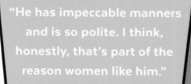

LOVE HiM

"He has impeccable manners and is so polite. I think, honestly, that's part of the reason women like him."

—an "insider" quoted in "Pete Davidson Tries 'Low Key' Dating Life After High-Profile Heartbreaks," *New York Post*, September 14, 2019

"He looks like a troll doll with a tapeworm."

—Rep. Dan Crenshaw (R-TX), "Weekend Update," *SNL*, November 10, 2018

HATE HiM

appeared to have been a civilized and no-hard-feelings breakup did not hurt his profile, either.[4]

Given the buzzy, attention-grabbing nature of Pete's later relationships, his first long-term one in the public eye was relatively quiet. In 2016, he started dating Larry David's daughter, writer and actor Cazzie David. That relationship pushed Pete into a new category. In some ways, he was the bigger star, given the growth of his *SNL* fanbase.

But while her media profile was far thinner—mostly creating and starring in the web series *Eighty-Sixed*, which Pete had a cameo in—she had credibility on Instagram, which she often filled with images of her and Pete being dreamy and in love. That took his social media presence away from just Funny Stoner Kid Who Does the Rap Vids on *SNL* and added an element of Quirky Dreamy Romantic Boyfriend.[5]

That may have helped Pete's chances when he met up with Ariana Grande in March 2018 when she came to an *SNL* after-party. At this time, Grande was one of the biggest music acts in the world. She headlined massive tours

---

4. "But how would people know how they broke up?" some men are wondering. This is because men frequently forget that women talk with each other after breakups. That means good news spreads fast. But so does the bad. Meaning: be careful, guys.

5. Pete was also clearly a Good Instagram Boyfriend, which is harder than you think. It involves angles, filters, and the patience to not eventually shout, "Fine, you take it!" and pout.

DATING UP TIP

Jealousy is unattractive. There is nothing to gain from resenting or competing with a more successful partner. Instead, simply bask in the benefits. As Pete said to Remy Smidt in a 2018 BuzzFeed News interview about his engagement to Ariana Grande, "I'm totally comfortable being with a successful woman. It's dope. I live at her place. She pays like 60 grand for rent, and all I have to do is stock the fridge."

and amassed fierce brigades of stans[6] who eagerly waged online battle with anybody they suspected for a second of disrespecting their queen. Meanwhile, Pete was still primarily seen as Stoner Kid on *SNL* Who Looks Like He's Twelve.[7]

---

6. From the Eminem song, i.e., a kind of superfan best avoided. In your grandparents' day, they screamed themselves hoarse at concerts. These days they're more likely to social-media bully somebody who only gave Beyoncé's last album 4.8 out of 5 stars.

7. Maybe thirteen. Perpetually young, this kid.

This meant he was definitely the one dating up. In a move that looked either intensely romantic or wildly impulsive, depending on how you look at it, Pete jumped right into things with Grande before quite fully untangling himself from his two-year relationship with David.

Messy? Yes. Things got messy later as well. But that mattered far less than the fact that Pete kept dating up. At some point, his celebrity status, which was part of what made him seem like dating material to women who were better known than him, began to increase in relation to the celebrities he was going out with.

Success breeds success.

Though the Grande relationship fell apart in Hemingway fashion[8]—moving from matching tattoos, engagement announcements, and a whole lot of Instagramming to breaking up in about six months—by the end of it, Pete had moved into an entirely different dating category. The details of his and Grande's breakup were very public and very complicated. But while the whole episode resulted in torrents of negativity from her and her stans (see "thank u, next"), it still meant that he had become A-list dateable.

Pete's dating success is largely due to his charm, humor, and heart. All strong qualities, but only valuable as a

---

8. "Gradually, then suddenly."—Ernest Hemingway's *The Sun Also Rises*, 1926

DOS AND DON'TS OF
DATING UP

DO keep your eyes, mind, and heart open. Tall, small, upbeat and perky, downbeat and sour, younger, older, there is no consistent discernible physical pattern to the women Pete has dated.

DON'T have a type. Some men have a tendency to focus on particular physical and personality factors, but women will likely not appreciate feeling that they fit the mold of someone's previous love interests or that they're in anything but a category of their own.

complete and comprehensive package, whether dating up, down, or sideways.

But there are other considerations. Especially when dating (or trying to date) people who have complicated, demanding, and unique professions that take up a lot of their time and isolate them from people. Like celebrities.

There is a reason that people who work in the same fields tend to pair up romantically. First is simply because it puts people in sustained close proximity to each other. Second, and particularly important to people working in arts and entertainment, it can be easier to not have to explain things about their work, which could impact a couple's time together.

After Pete dated Cazzie David, he probably knew better what it was like to travel in wealthy Hollywood circles. Once being acclimatized to the habits and traits of that class,[9] Pete could then be more at home with what daily life was like for an international pop star like Grande. Then, when Pete was sensitized to the Grande kind of lifestyle, and his fame had continued to rise, he could be viewed as a prospect by a wider range of celebrity women. He was, in a sense, already trained to deal with mega celebrity. He came with good qualifications and even references! Having dated the kind of women many perceived as out of his league and not having face-planted with an embarrassing breakup, he showed that he could fly close to the sun and not get burnt.

Post-Grande, Pete was something of a serial dater. He had a short relationship with actress Margaret Qualley (*Once Upon a Time ... in Hollywood*). He was linked as well for a time to actress Phoebe Dynevor (*Bridgerton*) and Cindy Crawford's daughter, model Kaia Gerber.

---

9. Per Cher Horowitz (*Clueless*), one example might be not needing to know how to parallel park because "everywhere you go has valet."

Viewed in the ever-shifting, hard-to-parse rankings of Hollywood, each of those women was roughly within Pete's orbit in terms of their level of fame. This showed that while he was not going out with noncelebrities, he

THE DOWNSIDES OF DATING UP

There are downsides to the high-profile dating life. Among the more high-ranking irritations would likely be paparazzi shouting things like, "Are you two breaking up?!" when you're just trying to get an iced coffee. Also having every single one of your relatives at Thanksgiving asking, "So ... what's she *really* like?" The top issue, though, might be the increased chances of having a stalker. If you read Nick Romano's *Entertainment Weekly* article from March 19, 2021, you'd know that a woman claimed she and Pete had married and were starting a production company together. She later broke into his house.

was also not consistently seeking out women who were a step up from himself.

Being plucked from the bottom rung by a pop star is endearing, but nobody likes a social climber.

At the same time, that did not stop Pete from occasionally making news by going out with women more famous than himself.

The news that he was going out with Kate Beckinsale right after things ended with Grande, though, was what broke many people's brains. That relationship also opened people's eyes to the possibility that Pete was something more than a goofy Staten Island guy who occasionally ensorcelled women who would normally be out of his range. It was one thing to date daughters of famous people or even pop stars who were roughly his age. It was quite another to date a woman who was twenty years his senior, a renowned actor (before the vampire/werewolf movies, at least), wicked smart,[10] and generally considered one of the most beautiful people in the world.

For Beckinsale, though, it was quite simple. According to the March 2, 2019, *People* magazine article by Maria Pasquini, she had a very specific response when asked by *Extra* about the kind of man she likes: "Funny. I like funny."

---

10. She's Oxford-educated, speaks Russian, and apparently, according to Andrew Court's October 22, 2021, *New York Post* article, has a 152 IQ.

Once Pete proved his ability to attract and stay with such an array of famous women, that essentially erased most limits to his potential dating pool.

Which is why, even though Megan Fox told him "never gonna happen" when Davidson made the gutsy move of asking for Kim Kardashian's number, he knew he still had a chance.

It had happened before.

CHAPTER 2

VULNERABLE IS THE NEW VIRILE

> ## "OFF THE TOP, I'M LIKE,
> ## 'HEY, I'M NUTS'
> ## … AND THAT CAN EITHER BE A LOT
> ## FOR SOMEONE … OR THEY COULD
> ## BE LIKE, 'COOL, THAT WAS REALLY
> ## REFRESHINGLY HONEST.'"
>
> —Pete Davidson, interview with *The Breakfast Club*, May 6, 2021

Lots of people have a type. A few stick to it and will not waver. Somewhere out in the world right now is a woman who is just really hoping to meet a guy with a shaved head and a slight lisp who can run a 5K and knows sign language.

Some prefer the strong, silent type. Face like a granite cliff. Eyes peering into the middle distance. Thinking of life, death, *fate*. Rationing out words like they were the last bullets in a desperate gunfight.

But you are reading a book about Pete Davidson. So it's unlikely the strong, silent type interests you.

And why would it? *Let's see, I'd like a guy who just kind of sits there, doesn't have a lot of opinions, shows no emotions, never clues me in to what he's thinking—much less, what he's feeling—but is willing to start a fight if I decide my honor needs protecting. Or something.* What about that sounds appealing? It's a pose.

Then there's the opposite end of the spectrum.

Emo guys don't keep their emotions inside. Their emotions overflow. For them, the dam is always breaking. That's why the eternal frown, the limp haircut, the softly pleading eyes. But this can seem just as much a pose as the strong, silent types. Ever see an emo guy giggle? Is that because he has literally never heard anything funny or because it's off-brand?

Pete falls somewhere in the middle.

Really, he's a talker type. He talks about all the things. He talks about his life, his feelings, his worries, and his various internal struggles with a straightforward and unfiltered honesty.

The kind of guy who jumps into relationships without reservations, he appears to go from zero to sixty in a matter of minutes whenever first getting together with a new somebody. He describes himself as a full-bore romantic, which certainly takes the edge off some of his intensity.[11]

As he would be the first to admit, this can be a lot to take in. It might also be a lot for a new girlfriend to get her arms around.

---

11. The jawline, puppy-dog eyes, and bad-boy grin don't hurt, either.

DATING UP TIP

Hang out your dirty laundry, all of it. Even the pink polka-dotted boxers. They're going to find out anyway.

At the same time, there is a certain genius to Pete's no-bullshit strategy.[12] It gets rid of the surprises. Any woman who would be, like, "byeee!" when finding out the real dirt on him has already been warned off.

Pete has said all the things out in public. So if you are a fabulously famous and wealthy actress/model/influencer, and you see on TMZ that Pete and his latest girlfriend are on the outs, you know all of his baggage before you have your assistant track down his number so you can send a coy, flirty text.

Before any of Pete's dates meet him for the first time, they know a few things:

- ♥ He has bravely shared that the defining trauma of his life was the horrible loss of his firefighter father on September 11th when Pete was only seven years old. He started performing stand-up comedy as a teenager in part to find a positive way to work through his sadness.

---

12. Assuming it is a strategy and not just, you know, *him*.

- Pete has also struggled with mental health issues for most of his life.
- He was diagnosed with borderline personality disorder (BPD) in 2017. All too familiar with anxiety, depression, and manic episodes, he has been working through it with therapy for a number of years.
- Diagnosed with Crohn's disease while still in high school, he started smoking pot to manage the symptoms. That ultimately led to more than one stint in drug rehabilitation.

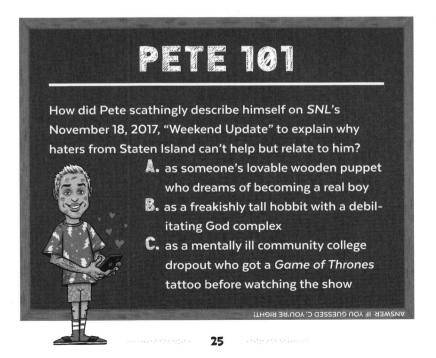

PETE 101

How did Pete scathingly describe himself on *SNL*'s November 18, 2017, "Weekend Update" to explain why haters from Staten Island can't help but relate to him?

A. as someone's lovable wooden puppet who dreams of becoming a real boy

B. as a freakishly tall hobbit with a debilitating God complex

C. as a mentally ill community college dropout who got a *Game of Thrones* tattoo before watching the show

ANSWER: IF YOU GUESSED C, YOU'RE RIGHT!

HUMBLE iN HOLLYWOOD

Often incorrectly lumped in with Hollywood's current crop of self-promoting twenty-something actor-bros, Pete exudes an insecurity that is so unique and raw that it makes you want to hug him. The night before shooting began on *The King of Staten Island*—a movie he was starring in and that  was based on his life—he emailed director and co-writer Judd Apatow a list of other actors who would be better at playing himself. *Who does that?*

As Davidson said, it's a lot. Like, a lot a lot.

Many men would keep much of that buried. For a while, at least.

But nothing ever stays buried. Despite what generations of men were told, or were expected to just instinctively know, trauma does not simply disappear after it is ignored for long enough. Things come to the surface, usually in the wrong way and at the wrong time, even when the guy is swearing up and down that nothing is wrong.[13]

---

13. "Seriously, I'm *fine!*"

Another way to describe that kind of behavior in a relationship is *emotional unavailability*. Some people find that kind of thing attractive, even sexy. But when they're being honest, they know it's a terrible idea.

Given Pete's hop-up-and-down romanticism, desire to put all his issues out there, and willingness to open himself up to a degree that is unusual even in the reality TV era, he could easily be described as emotionally available.

Some people would put that in opposition to the strong, silent type. But in reality, the guys who don't open up and never put anything of themselves out there in an honest fashion can appear self-protective and even possibly scared.

It takes real strength to show yourself, warts and all, in the way that Pete does. People who do that leave themselves open to all kinds of ugly, bullying behavior. It is not easy. Not every guy can do it. Too few of them try.

Pete throws himself to the wolves time and time again, but all it does is reveal him as a big, lovable puppy. After coming clean about his BPD,

DATING UP TIP

Forget everything other guys have told you about women. They love a guy with baggage. (Assuming that you are willing to unpack it at some point.)

Pete wrote the following in a May 24, 2018, Instagram story about still being in a relationship with Ariana Grande:

> "just because someone has a mental illness does not mean they can't be happy and in a relationship. it also doesn't mean that person makes the relationship toxic."

It would be one thing if Pete just opened up about his pain and difficulties and left it at that. He could have used those struggles as a crutch or an excuse for bad behavior. But that's not what he does. He explains his issues, tries to find a positive angle, and comes clean about how he is working on things. He also frequently takes it *way* too far.

With Pete, oversharing is a feature, not a bug.

Nothing about what he reveals and how he conducts himself is easy. It is not for the weak.

The strong, vulnerable type is a type that women don't always know to look

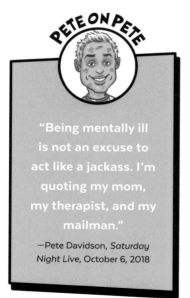

PETE ON PETE

"Being mentally ill is not an excuse to act like a jackass. I'm quoting my mom, my therapist, and my mailman."

—Pete Davidson, *Saturday Night Live*, October 6, 2018

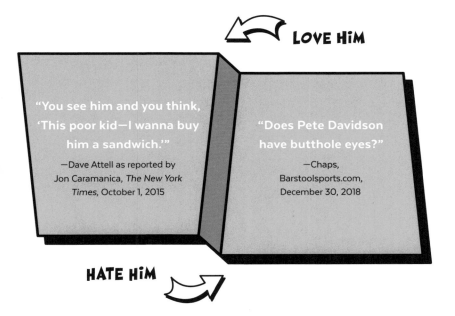

LOVE HiM

"You see him and you think,
'This poor kid—I wanna buy
him a sandwich.'"

—Dave Attell as reported by
Jon Caramanica, *The New York
Times*, October 1, 2015

"Does Pete Davidson
have butthole eyes?"

—Chaps,
Barstoolsports.com,
December 30, 2018

HATE HiM

for. They may not even realize its value as a highly date-able, boyfriend-worthy, category of men. But, as Pete has proven with his undisputed appeal to women the world over, including Hollywood royalty, it is pure gold when it comes to dating up.

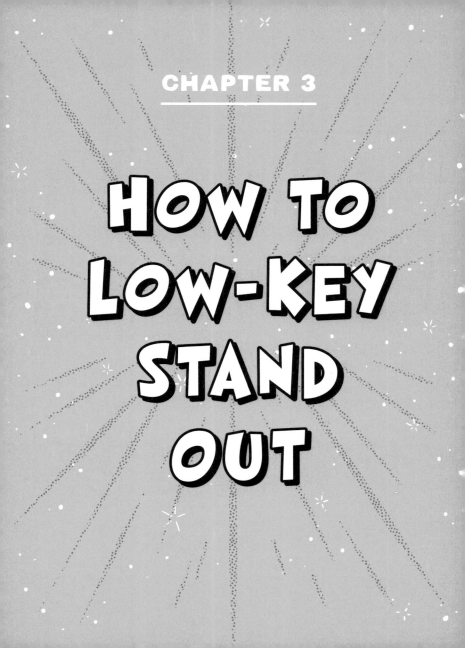

CHAPTER 3

HOW TO LOW-KEY STAND OUT

"IF YOU SEE SOMEONE WHO LOOKS LIKE THEY **JUST WOKE UP** AND **HASN'T SLEPT IN DAYS**, IT'S ME."

—Pete Davidson, "Weekend Update," *Saturday Night Live*, May 22, 2021

Some public figures can surf the peaks and crashes of an audience's attention by constantly changing things up and catching the next trend. Others stay in the spotlight through sheer consistency, by making themselves into a character who draws people in and adding slight variations over time.

Like many other comics, Pete had to find a way to stick in people's minds when he was just starting out. But rather than narrowing his act down to a very specific kind of comedy or (God forbid) a catchphrase, he created a persona that was in and of itself funny (and somehow also deeply attractive).

The greatest trick a comedian can pull is making an audience laugh without even telling a joke. This is a large part of Pete's appeal and a key to his success, both professionally and with women.

The greatest trick a skinny, tattooed kid from New York's lost borough with few marketable skills except for a sideways *wait, what?* kind of charm can pull off is to make himself memorable to people who would normally not give him a second glance.

When he was starting out, Pete needed something. It didn't need to be a big something, just something that made him different from all the borough guys trying to get a solid ten minutes of jokes about their girlfriends at the Comedy Cellar. Like Davidson's friend and fellow overly enthusiastic tattooer Machine Gun Kelly asked on November 27, 2011, in

DOS AND DON'TS OF
DATING UP

DO try to be yourself. Even when you are getting paid to act like someone else.

DON'T go beyond your limits. You know how actors will say on their resumes they can do a whole lot of things they really cannot (speak French, ride a horse, fence) so they can get the part, assuming they'll figure it out before shooting starts? Don't do that. The start of a new relationship is not the time to start pretending you speak French. Classic sitcom fail.

a Facebook post, "Why do we try so hard to fit in, when we are born to stand out?"

Pete might have known that the gimmick he landed on could bolster his career. But he probably had no idea it would make him a total snack in the eyes of Hollywood's hottest women.

In 2013, Pete had a brief appearance in the *Brooklyn Nine-Nine* episode "The Slump." He played Steven, a teenager disrupting a Scared Straight–type community outreach program with questions and creating a mocking, impromptu rap song with the instructor's own dialogue.

He's a class clown, but cute about it. The character he embodies is appealing because in that moment he comes across more as a kid who is playing around and being clever (making the song on the spot with his phone is a neat trick) rather than trying to be obnoxious. He's the boy who girls might want to actually talk with after class.

The character is on screen for just a few seconds, but he doesn't just blend into the ensemble. He stands out.

Pete's *Saturday Night Live* character the following year had echoes of Steven: underachieving, sleepy-eyed wiseass in hip-hop attire who looks to be about thirty seconds away from blazing up but has something to say. The characters he's played since have mostly been variations on that same character, with the only difference being that Pete ratchets the volume and intensity up or down.

When it came to Chad, the intensity was way, way down. Like a lot of new cast members, Pete didn't get a lot of play on his first season of SNL. But the second season, he started appearing in occasional digital shorts as Chad. A genially blank twenty-something with a fuzzy grasp of reality, Chad is put in a variety of increasingly extreme situations—from having an affair with a married Julia Louis-Dreyfus to being trapped in a Scream scenario—which never seem to affect him. His response to everything is a slightly bored but still agreeable, "Okay."

It is all right out of the Pete Davidson playbook.[14]

A common career route to fame for comics and comedic actors, in addition to stand-up, is grabbing TV and movie roles as they come. Literally anything, no matter whether it plays to their strengths or not. For example, early in his career, Jim Carrey played a vampire, sort of, in Once Bitten; funny it was not. Bill Hader, who shared a scene with Pete in the movie Trainwreck and helped him get the audition for SNL, had a bit on Punk'd where he made Ashlee Simpson cry—not attractive, not on-brand.

---

14. If there actually is a playbook, it is definitely one of those college-ruled notebooks that everybody had to get for school, beat to hell and littered with shake weed, only it doesn't have notes from geometry class, but rather analyses of Wu-Tang lyrics, ideas for new tattoos (e.g., Lorne Michaels as the angel on his shoulder), and bits for his next special. While it is certainly possible the playbook also has schematics laying out his 3-, 5-, and 10-year career plans (not to mention aspirational #girlfriendgoals), it seems far more likely that is not the case. One does not achieve Pete success by putting it all down on paper or screen.

This is not to criticize working comics. After all, the rent is due each month, headshots ain't free, and they don't hand out Screen Actors Guild health insurance to people without credits. Clearly, Carrey and Hader have done all right for themselves anyway.

But Pete is all about doing what works for him and what makes sense for him. Occasional "Weekend Update" bits where he basically riffs on his real-life persona (drugs, living at home, having anxiety). Funny loser dude in *Trainwreck*.

 **LOVE HiM**

"Obviously women find him very attractive. ... He seems super charming. He's vulnerable. He's lovely. His fingernail polish is awesome."

—Emily Ratajkowski, interview with *Vanity Fair*, November 10, 2021

"Pete Davidson always looks like a starving wolf in mid-transformation."

—"@MadMarkWolfmanChannel, YouTube comment, Pete Davidson's Comedy Central Stand-Up episode, September 28, 2019

 **HATE HiM**

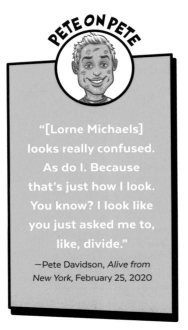

PETE ON PETE

"[Lorne Michaels] looks really confused. As do I. Because that's just how I look. You know? I look like you just asked me to, like, divide."

—Pete Davidson, *Alive from New York*, February 25, 2020

Significantly longer version of the funny loser dude in *The King of Staten Island*.

He also had the brains and the guts to take a role that others might have turned down. In 2021, he had received positive attention for *The King of Staten Island* and was just about the hottest thing going on *Saturday Night Live* (all the tabloid attention to his celebrity dating habits did not hurt). Then came word that he was going to be in one of that year's big comic-book movies, *The Suicide Squad*, only it was playing a character with a less-than-starring role.[15]

Nothing in these roles points to any sense of coolness, straining for approval, or over-the-top machismo. Which

---

15. *SPOILER ALERT* Blackguard turns out to be an unintelligent, traitorous dork who gets his face blown off just a few minutes into the movie. Not the kind of role that a lot of up-and-coming stars would take. But the character's comedic cluelessness might have appealed. Also, Pete reported that he took the role when offered by director James Gunn because the character's real name was Dick Hertz.

is for the best, since those are all qualities possessed by many guys at his age, famous or not, and none of them are enjoying his epic level of dating success.

You could say that Pete sticking to a narrow lane sug-gests a limited skill set. Or maybe a lack of confidence in his own abilities.

Really, though, isn't it just smart? Also self-aware?

There are plenty of guys jumping up and down trying to get your attention. It's what they do.

Then there are the ones like Pete. They know who they are and what they can (and cannot) do.

It's not a hard choice.

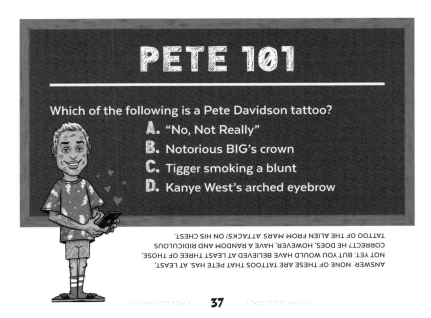

PETE 101

Which of the following is a Pete Davidson tattoo?

A. "No, Not Really"

B. Notorious BIG's crown

C. Tigger smoking a blunt

D. Kanye West's arched eyebrow

ANSWER: NONE OF THESE ARE TATTOOS THAT PETE HAS. AT LEAST, NOT YET. BUT YOU WOULD HAVE BELIEVED AT LEAST THREE OF THOSE, CORRECT? HE DOES, HOWEVER, HAVE A RANDOM AND RIDICULOUS TATTOO OF THE ALIEN FROM MARS ATTACKS! ON HIS CHEST.

CHAPTER 4

HOW TO DRESS UGLY HOT

"SHE DIDN'T LET ME WEAR MY PROPELLER HAT, BUT IT'S FINE."

—Pete Davidson, on coordinating with Kim Kardashian at the 2022 Met Gala, *Harper's Bazaar*, May 2, 2022

There are lists of best-dressed celebrities and the worst dressed. While Pete is unlikely to end up on the first list, he could not in good conscience be added to the second. There are a lot of wardrobe fails in his time in the spotlight. As he once pointed out while showing a picture of himself in a huge purple Kangol hat and sleeveless Bathing Ape T-shirt, the shirt was only "the second stupidest thing" he had on. But his fashion sense has matured during his time in the spotlight, enough to where the women he is with can worry less about what he is going to wear but not so much that he is paying more attention to his outfits than they are to theirs.

The boyfriend fashion sweet spot, in other words.

We all know that what's on the inside is what matters. Right? All those surface attributes are not what's important. You don't go out with a face, or a body, or a wardrobe; you go out with a person. The measure of that person is the content of their heart, their mind, their soul.

That is completely true.

But ...

If you are going out with a guy who happens to have a great heart, mind, soul, what have you, is it too much to ask that he not leave the house looking like something that your diabetic cat just hacked up on your 300-count sheets?

Pete has mastered the alluring art of looking like he doesn't know how to dress. And this strategy is working. In a July 18, 2019, "Dressing Funny" episode on Netflix Is a Joke, *Queer Eye*'s Tan France discovers that Pete hasn't really thought about what looked cool since he was 18 (which appeared to be manga T-shirts and jean jackets?), saying that the best approximation for his style sensibility was "guido trash." There was also a moment when he said (maybe serious, maybe not) his fashion icon was Adam Sandler (sweatpants, hoodies, nothing constricting).

In other words, not the kind of guy you could imagine

PETE ON PETE

"I dress how I dressed when I was like 10. I'm, like, 'What would be cool? Purple pants.'"

—Pete Davidson, *GQ*, August 16, 2018

bringing out anywhere unless you had a serious wardrobe conversation first. Which nobody wants to have to do.[16]

But despite what Pete claims—not to mention those admittedly Barney-ish zip-ups he would wear on "Weekend Update" and that really unfortunate mustache that made him look like a biker who didn't make it into the gang—he not only knows how to dress, he is actually aware there is a thing called fashion that men are allowed to dabble in.

It has taken him a little time to get to that point, though.

Remember the Ariana Grande "lusty lollipop" photo? In some ways, that was not a bad look. In the picture, she makes a statement, with her canary yellow pullover hoodie-as-dress and thigh-high boots complementing that *look* she gives him while licking a sucker and walking hand-in-hand. She probably didn't mind being the gravitational center of that picture. Given that he may have just been running through an H&M yanking things off the shelf, his style gets a passing grade—running pants, T-shirt from a Robert Pattinson movie, button-up flannel over a black sweatshirt with the hood up, and sucker stick poking out.

You don't need your boyfriend to look like he has been primping all day. You just need him to dress down and let you shine.

16. "Is that what you're wearing?" having been voted Question Most Likely to Start an Argument with Your Significant Other by *Relationships Should Not Be This Complicated* magazine.

More recently, Pete started making an effort, but not too much of one. This reveals four important things: First, he understands clothes matter. Second, somebody likely told him that he needed to step up his fashion game and he *listened*.[17] Third, he puts together a look but doesn't invest an unseemly amount of effort into its planning (after a fashion shoot for the magazine, *GQ* writer Allie Jones revealed in her August 16, 2018, article "The Adventures of Pete Davidson" that since Davidson has "the swagger of a Staten Island dice roller" and doesn't exactly lay out his outfits the night before, they "ditched the rack and embarked on a sartorial Choose Your Own Adventure"). Fourth, he still generally dresses down enough so that he is not taking attention away from the women he's with.

In the beginning of this new phase, he specialized in the kinda-paying-attention-but-looking-like-I'm-not streetwear thing that younger male celebs out and about in New York will try. A lot of skateboarder-adjacent threads from Supreme, track pants, pops of randomized color from tie-dyed Grateful Dead T-shirts or hot pink sweatshirts, and a wide array of sneakers heavy on Vans and snow-white Adidas with the occasional over-the-top set of kicks ($1,200 Air Jordan 2s). He was not just some bro throwing on whatever

---

17. Neither being traits generally associated with attention-seeking men in their twenties.

he had and sticking to glum and basic monochromes, usually. The outfits hit that sweet spot of appearing casual but still purposeful and coordinated; again, *usually*.[18]

There was a time when people looking for a trend threw Pete in with some other younger actors with more baroque tastes. The whole "scumbro" anti-fashion fashion trend exemplified by the likes of Jonah Hill, Shia LaBeouf, and Justin Bieber had some streetwear overlap with Pete. But what the scumbros were throwing down was way more purposefully flamboyant and messy[19] than what Pete was going for.

Sometime in the post-Grande era of his dating life, when he was spotted with a steady list of actors and models, Pete began upping his clothing game. He started adding more designer names into his outfits. At premieres or red-carpet events, he began wearing blazers and chic shades, trying out a look that was more *upscale indie rocker* or *critically acclaimed actor* than *jumped-up Staten Island guy on the make.*

Pete then took it up a notch again. He got a stylist and even became a model himself, walking the runway for Alexander Wang's spring 2020 show in a shruggingly casual manner that said a lot about his confidence in the moment.

---

18. There were still definitely a lot of basketball shorts in the mix. It was a work in progress.

19. Think color-blind stoner with a platinum card.

UGLY HOT
FASHION TIP

Just because you have it doesn't mean you have to wear it. In the February 28, 2020, article "Pete Davidson Takes Fans on a Tour of His Basement Apartment in His Mom's House," *Us* magazine writer Johnni Macke gets an inside look at Pete's place in Staten Island. During the tour, he showed off a lot of things, from a graffiti wall for visitors to sign, 9/11 mementos, and his bedroom, "where *nothing happens*," he noted, "because I live with my mom." Stopping at his wall of sneakers, he pointed out a few pairs that were SpongeBob collectibles—he's quite the fan and has a tattoo of the show's character Plankton—before lamenting that he can never wear them "because they don't go with anything, except maybe yellow." It's important to set a few fashion standards, no matter how low they are.

At one point in 2021, he took over Calvin Klein's Instagram account.

But it was the 2021 Met Gala that really set Pete apart and put him on the way to becoming a true celebrity boyfriend. The fact that he was even invited and *wanted to attend* says a lot. A paparazzi-stalked red-carpet fashion showcase masquerading as a fundraiser, the Met Gala would likely be one of the most intensely boring nights out for many guys Pete's age. But when the opportunity came, he not only went, but he went in style. No BAPE T-shirts or Crocs this time.

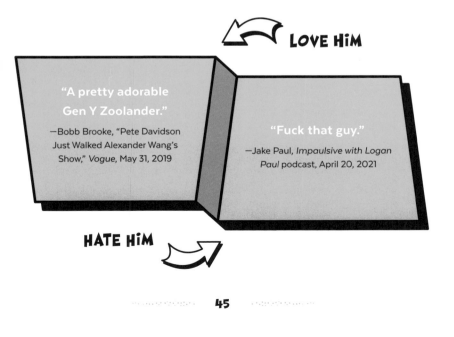

LOVE HiM

"A pretty adorable Gen Y Zoolander."

—Bobb Brooke, "Pete Davidson Just Walked Alexander Wang's Show," *Vogue*, May 31, 2019

"Fuck that guy."

—Jake Paul, *Impaulsive with Logan Paul* podcast, April 20, 2021

HATE HiM

It was a daring look, and what woman doesn't like a man who takes a chance? Designer Thom Browne's outfit was a knee-length black tunic dress with white overcoat and black boots, neatly accented by his dyed blonde hair and vintage jewelry, which was in honor of his father (the lapel pins and necklace had garnets, his father's birthstone).

There was mockery, of course. Some of it from Pete himself on the October 3, 2021, "Weekend Update," clearly comfortable in the moment and exhibiting zero touchiness:

> "I look like James Bond at his quinceañera. I look like if one of the Three Blind Mice sold fentanyl … I look like Tilda Swinton on casual Friday."

Pete kept mixing it up in a high-low, out-there fashion sense. The same year, he went on Jimmy Fallon wearing New Balance sneakers, flower-print jeans, and a purple cardigan over a cat T-shirt, very much looking like he just raided a hippie grandmother's closet ("Babetastic Fashion Bro" was another hot take from Liana Satenstein in her September 9, 2021, *Vogue* article).

What it all comes down to is that Pete knows how to dress in a way that reflects his unique personality. But at the same time, he is not trying to outshine anybody by being the prettiest peacock out there. That is the sweet spot for a woman looking to date and be photographed with him.

Find the right fashion balance that works for you. Dress like you intended to look the way you do and didn't just grab some stuff off the floor. Own your fashion choices, no matter how bad somebody else might think they are. And never, ever dress better than your date.

If you were to piece together his erratic fashion rules, you might start with these:

❤ Get a decent-size wardrobe: Pete is often wearing new items people have not seen before. This means he is used to buying clothes, switching things out, and having a lot to choose from. This means that when his girl buys him a shirt that she thinks will go great with his eyes, he may actually put it into rotation rather than just wearing it once to make her happy.

❤ Don't be afraid to wear nail polish: Every so often, Pete will be seen with painted nails, like the time he went to a Knicks game flashing bright red nail polish. Often, it's not even as part of a look. He is just wearing whatever he normally would and, oh yeah, he's got nail polish on. It might be different if he was primping and constantly getting manicures. But the casual, *why not?* nature of it shows a guy who is highly confident and couldn't care less what haters might say. (He could also just be shilling for his buddy Machine Gun Kelly, who has his own nail polish brand.)

♥ Take risks with color: Unlike a lot of guys, he isn't afraid of color. Pinks, yellows, purples, they're all in the mix. That widens the possibilities of what he will wear when going out. It also means that if his date wants him to switch things up to not clash with her outfit, he has more options.

♥ Dress with your date in mind: When he and Kim Kardashian had their first red-carpet event as a couple, attending the 2022 White House Correspondents' Dinner, he kept it stylish and cool but subtle: black Prada suit and skinny black tie, with black Vans for a dash of something different. This ensured all eyes were on her and that silver Balenciaga mermaid dress with the liquid shine, which is what every boyfriend should want.

- Know your designer labels: This is key. The kind of women Pete dates are very familiar with designer labels. A number of them have been paid to represent different fashion houses. They will like a guy who doesn't think Gucci or Versace is just a word rappers throw in to fill out a verse.
- Be taller: No, height (Pete is 6'3") shouldn't have anything to do with fashion. But it can help you stand out and make an entrance.

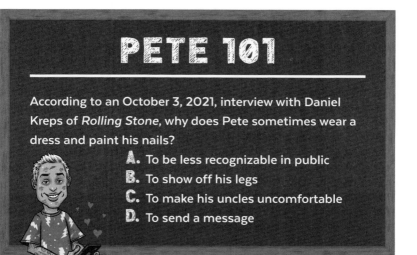

PETE 101

According to an October 3, 2021, interview with Daniel Kreps of *Rolling Stone*, why does Pete sometimes wear a dress and paint his nails?

A. To be less recognizable in public
B. To show off his legs
C. To make his uncles uncomfortable
D. To send a message

ANSWER: C. DAVIDSON'S UNCLE STEVE CHOOSES TO TAKE IT IN STRIDE, THOUGH. "ALL RIGHT, YOU'RE STILL WELCOME IN MY HOUSE," HE SAID TO PETE. "I'LL JUST PUT THE SEAT DOWN WHEN YOU'RE OVER."

> "EVEN THOUGH HIS SHTICK IS THAT **HE'S KIND OF A FUCK-UP**, HE ACTUALLY HANDLES HIMSELF WITH SUCH GRACE. ... **HE'S LOVELY.**"
>
> —Glenn Close, as reported on Todayonline.com, May 5, 2022

We have all seen the movies where a big-city girl moves back home to the country and falls in love with the local veterinarian. And the will-they-or-won't-they TV shows where employed adults with an unlikely amount of downtime meet up in cafés for whole days to exchange spicy barbs about relationships. Rom-coms are predictable. But they still satisfy and soothe and suggest that something better is attainable.

Anyone who understands the structure of a romantic comedy understands something about Pete's appeal.

He is not a romantic lead. Not in the traditional sense. He does not have that aspirational, clean-cut, smart-bet boyfriend material vibe that often gets paired on a movie poster with whoever the hot A-list blonde of the moment is. Nothing about the personality he presents to the world represents killing-it confidence.

DOS AND DON'TS OF
DATING UP

DO surprise her with an endless, confusing whirl-wind of self-deprecation.

DON'T be afraid to hide in the friend zone for as long as it takes.

That is because in the romantic comedy, he would play the "Just Friends" guy flying under the radar. Until the leading lady finally saw that he was the one who "got" her, just when she was having doubts about the guy who everyone said was perfect for her. Then he'd get the girl.

Key to the appeal of this character is underplaying the appeal. In fact, Pete seems to go out of his way to undercut himself.

This is an old stand-up trick. He probably used it a lot when first getting up onstage at the Looney Bin.[20] Many comics with a physical attribute that they think the audience

---

20. A Staten Island comedy club that was also a bowling alley. Not an ideal spot for launching an international comedy career. Which makes his unlikely climb to the A(-ish)-list even more impressive.

is going to seize on will start off with jokes at their expense, which shows they're not taking themselves too seriously.

That helps lower barriers. One of the most attractive aspects of Pete's personality is how few barriers he seems to put up. There does not seem to be an easy way for somebody else to successfully insult him about his dress, physique, life choices, or anything else. For the most part, anything negative that somebody else wants to say about Pete, he has already said about himself.

Pete's enthusiasm for making fun of himself is essential to his Ugly Hot appeal. For instance, here are just a few of the jokes Pete has made about his own appearance:

- "[I look like a] crack baby."
  —as reported by the *New York Post*, November 4, 2021

- "I should inspire hope that literally anyone can be on *Saturday Night Live*. Seriously, you see a guy bumming cigarettes outside a 7-Eleven at 2 a.m., that's not some meth head, that's the next Pete Davidson!"
  —*Saturday Night Live*, May 21, 2022

- "I'm 6'3", 140 pounds, I kind of look like I should be outside a car dealership, flapping in the wind."
  —as reported by nj.com, April 12, 2016

- "If I'm the type of guy that your daughter or mother is into, then trust me, I'm the best-case scenario.

There are a million guys who look like me, and I'm the only one with a job."
—*Saturday Night Live*, December 21, 2019

Given that level of self-criticism, it is easy for women to believe that he will be painfully honest and trustworthy in a relationship. Guys who care that little about putting up a front just seem less likely to create elaborate scenarios for deception.[21]

Pete's self-deprecating jokes might suggest that he thinks he's a loser. But his confidence contradicts that theory. What seems more likely is that he appreciates just how far he has come and how unlikely his success is. What is more attractive? A puffed-up guy with good looks and some coin but the self-awareness of a designer T-shirt?[22] Or a guy who comes on like a real person and lets *you* discover what he's got going on?

Like most comics who attain worldwide popularity but downplay their own coolness, looks, and intelligence, Pete seems to have a decent understanding of some aspects of his appeal. At the Patrice O'Neal Comedy Benefit Concert on January 18, 2022, he compared himself to the piles of discount DVDs that you might find at a 7-Eleven, with movies

---

21. After all, not many men can pull off occasional heavy weed intake while simultaneously maintaining complicated lies without giggling or staring blankly at inappropriate times.
22. Which really does seem like a cheat, right? How much can you design a plain T-shirt anyway?

like *Shrek Forever After* or *Tropic Thunder*. He argued that some of those movies didn't actually deserve to be in the markdown bin, joking that "I'm *Tropic Thunder*. I'm the diamond in the trash. It's a steal."

In a May 21, 2022, "Weekend Update" appearance, Pete explained why he was so amazed by the career he managed to have: "I never imagined this would be my life. Back then, I was just a skinny kid that no one knew which race I was. And now everyone knows I'm white because I became hugely successful while barely showing up to work. Look at me now, I'm aging like an old banana."

What he is doing here is navigating that tricky middle ground between humility and bold confidence known as self-awareness. Humility is among the rarest and most appealing aspects of his public persona. Many of us could boost our value in the dating world and our likability by

PETE ON PETE

"I am just very, very honest. I think what a lot of people do is they try to put on ... almost like a version of themselves that they would like to be. And then eventually, that will unravel."

—Pete Davidson in an interview with *The Breakfast Club*, May 6, 2021

taking his approach to remaining resolutely unimpressed with ourselves.

Many celebrities get through the endless rounds of rejection necessary to attain their level of success by putting on a kind of armor. Not letting it look as though anything gets to them is their way of coping with all the negativity.

Pete appears to do the opposite and invite everything in.

When Kristen Stewart hosted *Saturday Night Live* on November 2, 2019, she took questions from cast members pretending to be audience members during her monologue. Pete put up his hand and said, "Ask me anything. I'm an open book. I put it all out there."

"Yes, you *will*," she answered knowingly.

There is also potentially a canny angle to much of Pete's persona building. His carefully constructed celebrity profile—well-publicized bouts of therapy and rehab, along with a tumultuous dating history—is one that absolutely lowers expectations. The tabloids are definitely expecting him to have a very public flaming-out. In fact, they're hoping for it.

Pete has faced a lot of obstacles in his career, especially his mental health and unwanted social media sniping. But there is little evidence that the persona he projects of a clueless, Xbox-playing, generally stoned kid—who not so long ago was just another one of the random guys performing mediocre comedy rap battles on *Wild 'n Out* and having opinions on *Guy Code*[23]—is really the whole story.

Pete would not have become the youngest cast member on *Saturday Night Live* if that was truly the case. He has been performing in comedy clubs since he was sixteen (an age when most comics can barely tell a joke yet, much less do so in front of a couple dozen bored

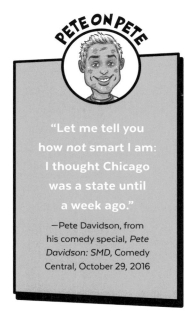

PETE ON PETE

"Let me tell you how *not* smart I am: I thought Chicago was a state until a week ago."

—Pete Davidson, from his comedy special, *Pete Davidson: SMD*, Comedy Central, October 29, 2016

strangers while bowling pins crash in the background). He clearly has an impressive work ethic—otherwise, how did he snag all those credits at a young age? He also knows how to make connections—otherwise, why did people like Amy Schumer, Bill Hader, and Lorne Michaels keep looking out for him?

---

23. No idea, either. Apparently it was a show on MTV2 where dude comics discussed dude things? It lasted five seasons. *Five.*

The persona he presents onstage, his "just friends" appeal, can also serve as convenient camouflage when it comes to the game of attraction.

In a romantic comedy, Pete would *not* be the first person the leading lady would notice. He would be off to the side, providing good advice and support, jokes when needed (maybe a puff off his joint), and surprising her in a way that the obvious guy with the nicer clothes, cleaner haircut, safe six-figure income, and serenely untroubled mental state never could.

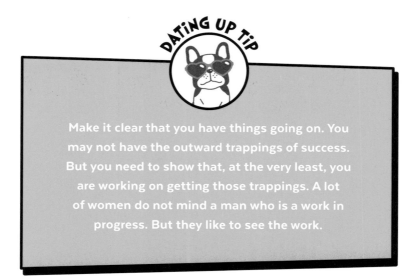

DATING UP TIP

Make it clear that you have things going on. You may not have the outward trappings of success. But you need to show that, at the very least, you are working on getting those trappings. A lot of women do not mind a man who is a work in progress. But they like to see the work.

Too many men make the mistake of trying to be the obvious guy. They don't understand that aiming for the obvious-guy lane means going up against a lot of competition. It also assumes that the woman they are trying to attract is shallow, deeply unoriginal, and does not want a romantic-comedy ending.

Pete projects approachable qualities that are appealing not just because they fit

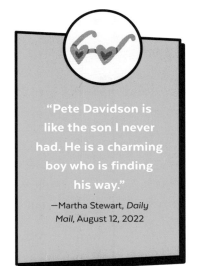

"Pete Davidson is like the son I never had. He is a charming boy who is finding his way."

—Martha Stewart, *Daily Mail*, August 12, 2022

into some calculated ideal presented by romantic comedies (though that does not hurt). What makes his personality so enticing is his openness about failure, willingness to mock himself for those failures, and acknowledgment of how unlikely he was to have any success at all. A man who knows all those things appears significantly less likely to judge the person they are with. Don't sleep on Pete's high-success strategy for getting an A-lister's attention. He's good.

Sneaky good.

"HE'S LIKE YOUR WEED DEALER WHOM YOU FEEL SAFE AROUND FOR SOME REASON, AND WHEN HE STARTS **CRACKING JOKES**, YOU REALIZE YOU'D HOOK UP WITH HIM."

—user icphx95 on the December 11, 2021, Reddit thread, "People who are attracted to Pete Davidson, why?"

It has been said countless times before, but many, many men have chosen not to listen. So here it is again: Women ~~like~~ love a man with a sense of humor. This isn't just something that people say, it's also backed up by science. Just about every major study conducted on what women find attractive shows that being funny is near the top of the list, if not at the top.

Comedians like Susan Prekel know this. In the October 1, 2012, *Scientific American* article "The Humor Gap," Prekel said she had only once been asked out after performing a set. But according to her, male comics "do very well with women."

(CONTINUED ON PAGE 64)

THE SCIENCE

Trust science. Multiple studies over the years have shown that men who make a woman laugh are more likely to be seen as viable romantic partners and somebody with whom they can imagine establishing a relationship (Ben-Zeév 2021). In one study that clearly predated the app era, men described as humorous were almost twice as likely to obtain phone numbers from women than men who were not (Geher and Kaufman 2013).

There are a lot of potential reasons for this, though researchers being researchers, they tend to ignore the obvious (funny is just more enjoyable to be around than dour and serious). One suggested reason was that humor is a sign of intelligence. While this is difficult to measure in a lab setting, the same point was reiterated in a July 23, 2022, E! News interview by Maria Bakalova (who co-starred with Pete in the horror film *Bodies Bodies Bodies*). She couldn't help but speak to his

OF PETE

brainpower when she praised his self-deprecating sense of humor: "Sarcasm, self-irony is a sign of intelligence." As much as Pete has downplayed or even dismissed the very existence of his mental agility, the pointedness of his comedy proves that wheels are turning behind that deceptively goofy smile.

Also, do not discount the wisdom of popular magazines that make the connection between humor and attractiveness over and over again for a reason (hint: because it's true).[24]

---

24. Men should know this as well. At least the ones who read *Men's Health*. According to Andrew Daniels in the March 1, 2013, article "Why Chicks Dig Funny Guys," *Men's Health* magazine polled 1,000 American women and found that over three-fourths of the respondents believed the absolutely most crucial personality trait in a potential mate was a "sense of humor." Only about half really cared how intelligent he was.

DOS AND DON'TS OF
DATING UP

DO Be organic. Try to find the humor in ordinary situations. See what makes her laugh. Do more of that.

DON'T Treat a date like an actual comedy act. No woman ever told her girlfriends, "It was a great date! He did this ten-minute bit on cocktail napkins!"

Pete is not just funny, he is the right *kind* of funny. For the most part, he is not the kind of comedian who breaks subjects down in a way that leads to enlightenment. His humor is approachable funny, personal funny, and quite often immature funny.

Most of his jokes work because of his delivery and the personality he brings to the bit.

In his February 25, 2020, special *Alive from New York*, Pete tells a story about how after his father died, the family received a settlement for families of 9/11 victims. His mother wanted to do something nice for him and his little sister, so she bought them a pool. Pete marvels at how other kids at school told him how lucky he was. He describes his response as, "Yeah, I'm lucky to have a pool ... that I *fill up with tears every summer.*"

On paper, this is not that funny. But in the special, it kills because of his presence, the slightly hushed voice, the edge that comes from painful memory, and the little wicked grin at the uncomfortable laughter that follows.

Another comedian might not have been able to sell that joke. It could have come off as either self-pitying or cruel. But because Pete carries himself with that winning, slightly anxious vulnerability, the bit registers as truth-telling.

To get an idea of how people fell for Pete, just take a look back at his time on *Saturday Night Live*. For years, he appeared on the show only rarely.[25] But then he started making regular appearances on "Weekend Update." Popping up next to Colin Jost or Michael Che, who play the scene as though they were his long-suffering older brothers indulging him, Pete gave his take on whatever might be going on at the moment. They could range from the Gawker/Hulk Hogan sex tape settlement to the trans bathroom ban and Donald Trump's cabinet picks, and he played off his under-achieving-kid shtick to make it relatable.

---

25. Lorne Michaels cast him at twenty years old, even though he did not have signature bits, self-admittedly could not act, and did not do impressions.

The material was rarely groundbreaking. His goofy glee in just performing made the jokes that much more enjoyable.

The "Weekend Update" moments where Pete is batting lines back and forth with Jost demonstrate the kind of humor that makes him particularly attractive. Even though at the moment he was likely the bigger star than Jost, Pete makes himself out to be the loser with jokes like this from the December 21, 2019, airing:

> "It's not fair, Colin. You get to date a famous woman [Scarlett Johansson] and everyone's delighted, but when I do it, the world wants to punch me in the throat?"

Who doesn't love an underdog?

Pete also threads issues with his mental health through this material. In the middle of a bit in which he is complaining about not getting enough airtime and passively aggressively suggesting having more of his sketches on air could help with his depression, he admits that won't happen since most of the bits he writes for himself are terrible: "They're written by a depressed person!" he adds on the October 8, 2017, "Weekend Update" with a self-deprecating twinkle.

A key pointer guys can pick up from Pete, one of those things you would think everybody knows but somehow they don't, is that humor can help difficult subjects go down easier. In one *SNL* bit on March 8, 2018, Pete talks about the praise NBA player Kevin Love received for an article he wrote about having a panic attack during a game. It's close to a textbook example of how to embed a vulnerable personal truth inside a joke: "If you're gonna write an article about being unstable, leave it to the big boys, all right? I'm sorry you missed your three-pointer, *Kev*, but I've been in therapy since I was six years old."

While being funny is key, that alone cannot explain the number of women longingly scrolling through their feeds for new Pete pics. There are a lot of funny men out there

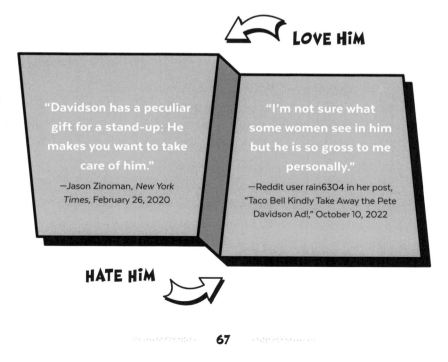

LOVE HiM

"Davidson has a peculiar gift for a stand-up: He makes you want to take care of him."

—Jason Zinoman, *New York Times*, February 26, 2020

"I'm not sure what some women see in him but he is so gross to me personally."

—Reddit user rain6304 in her post, "Taco Bell Kindly Take Away the Pete Davidson Ad!," October 10, 2022

HATE HiM

DOS AND DON'TS OF
DATING UP

DO get a job that surrounds you with jaw-droppingly attractive models, actresses, and celebs.

DON'T ever stop being funny. Funny makes you interesting and, even if you are already attractive, makes you much hotter.

who garner less excitement and support from women and fans. If word got out that Pete was shirtless on a beach with his girlfriend, paparazzi would be staked out nearby with telephoto lenses to get the picture.

Nobody is doing that for Kevin Hart, Dave Chappelle, or Bill Burr.[26]

Visibility is also important. Older, more successful comedians are more likely to be married and have children. That takes them off the dating scene. Pete was born in 1993 and lived with his mother for a significant part of his twenties, so

---

26. No offense.

public awareness of him as a single male was minimal until he broke into entertainment. During his many seasons on *Saturday Night Live*, for those weeks when he actually came into work, he had the opportunity to meet up with many famous women: Ariana Grande, Miley Cyrus, Kim Kardashian. They all came through studio 8H. And there Pete was.

"An amazing distraction."

—Ariana Grande on meeting Pete, *Vogue*, July 9, 2019

Not just a funny guy, because 30 Rock was filled with them.[27] But here was a funny guy with a boyish energy that came across as buoyant and playful instead of immature, like an Adam Sandler. A funny guy who is significantly less height-challenged than most other funny guys.

If not for comedy, how else would Pete have been seen as a prospect?

Jokes matter.

---

27. For a certain kind of woman, just getting in the door there must be like what other women would feel like at a cocktail bar filled with investment bankers and surgeons. Call it Laughter Goggles.

"GOD SAVED ME FROM
THAT CRASH JUST SO I CAN
BEAT PETE DAVIDSON'S ASS."

—Kanye West, "Eazy" (2022)

According to many informed sources, including Sara Nathan's March 3, 2022, Page Six *New York Post* article, in a certain music video made by a certain artist for a certain song, all of which shall remain nameless, the certain artist is shown beheading and burying alive a man who looks something like Pete.

So, as they say, that happened.

This took place in the early days of Pete and Kim Kardashian's relationship, which was a tabloid free-for-all. Every social media network seemed about to implode under the strain of transmitting tens of millions of posts expressing various strong reactions to seeing the comic and reality TV entrepreneur being ... *friendly* in public places.

That would be a lot of strain for any relationship to take—except Kardashian, of course, for whom online buzz is akin to oxygen—but Pete seemed to take it in stride, not talking a lot to the press but also not running from the cameras. Of

DATING UP TIP

Whatever her ex says or does, remember that there is a reason she *used to be* with him and is *now* with you. Everything else is noise.

course, outwardly Pete tends to take most things in stride. He's a stoner.

So far, so not helpful for the average reader. Navigating the paparazzi with your new girlfriend at Knott's Berry Farm[28] is not a problem for most people.

However it is fairly common to be in a new relationship where one of the ex-partners is not so willing to let things go and move on with their lives. In those situations, the ex-boyfriend or ex-girlfriend can make things very uncomfortable for the person they believe has replaced them. Phone calls. Surprise pop-bys. Passive-aggressive Facebook posts. Or, in Pete's case, a song posted to the Internet for the world to see in which the replacement person is symbolically murdered and buried.

Nevertheless, Pete's reaction to the anger directed his way by Kardashian's ex-husband Kanye West (who later

28. Apparently an amusement park and not just a place to go and pick berries? Does anybody outside Southern California know this? In any case, if this was their first real outing together, it is an appealingly untraditional choice.

went by Ye) remains instructive. Because Pete, for the most part, did not take the bait. He publicly resisted attempts by people to get him to be a combatant in a clickbait celebrity spat. There was every incentive for him to get into it with West. But he held back.

When Pete finally did respond to West was after the rapper made critical comments about Kardashian's parenting. By choosing that moment to push back a little, Pete showed that it was not all about him. Given the amount of bullying Pete faced as a child and his habit of cutting himself down to size at every possible opportunity, it seems apparent that there was not much West could say to Pete that would truly bother him. That level of self-acceptance and calm control is beyond what many men twice Pete's age can manage, even at the urging of their partner.

In an apparent text exchange between the two men that a friend of Pete's (Dave Sirus) made public on Instagram and then deleted, Pete praised Kardashian's skills as a mother. Then, according to Abigail Adams's account in *People* magazine on March 3, 2022, Pete laid into West, telling the star producer/rapper/mogul (who was sixteen years his senior) to "grow the [deleted] up." Pete tried to argue that there was no reason for them to fight, even claiming to have kept *SNL* from doing skits or jokes about West for months: "I have your back."

THE SCIENCE OF PETE

One study found that men tended to fight over women less to win a new romantic partner than to show their dominance over other men (Ainsworth and Maner 2012). There was some indication that the men in the study were driven to assert themselves over perceived male rivals out of the belief (conscious or not) that showing their dominance in this way would help them attract women. In other words, it has little or nothing to do with the woman herself or what she wants. That has never stopped men from trying to show dominance. In an anthropological study of Neolithic-era tribes in Europe, researchers discovered evidence that men might have been engaging in actual combat over women, who were almost certainly not polled by the combatants for their preferences (Durham University 2008). While the means of this kind of fighting has changed in the intervening millennia, the unattractiveness of it has not.

So far, so mature.

Then at one point in the back-and-forth, West asks Pete where he is, and the reply comes back, "in bed with your wife."

This did not help matters, but a person can only control himself for so long.

But somehow, even despite a few very ill-advised missteps, Pete still manages to come across as the more grown-up party in the exchange. Granted, this may not have been the most challenging accomplishment, given that the man on the other side of the equation once said to *The Fader* in December 2008, "I am God's vessel. But my greatest pain in life is that I will never be able to see myself perform live," is the same man who tweeted a fake headline announcing Pete's death.

After West kept inviting Pete to Sunday Service,[29] Pete turned him down, explaining quite rationally, "This isn't public dude." Pete went further, trying to make a connection with West about his own struggles with mental health, telling him, "There's no shame" in getting help.

Taking the high road is nearly always the best policy. As is de-escalation.

---

29. West's weekly gospel choir concerts that attracted flocks of celebrities and press. Perhaps not ideal for the calm settling of a personal beef?

Assuming that all this actually occurred in the way it was later reported,[30] the text exchange suggests Pete had very little interest in a showdown (public or private) with West. Given everything else we have seen with Pete, this makes sense. Nothing about his personality, the things he talks about, or even the way he holds himself onstage suggests a man who is looking to throw down outside a bar after closing.

Additionally, any man as willing to mock himself as Pete is will simply never be that susceptible to reacting angrily to another man's insults. What could any guy say to him that he has not already said about himself? Or worse?

If Pete had decided to go after West, even to defend Kardashian, it is unlikely that she would have been impressed.

While there is a stereotype out there that women always enjoy it when men fight over them, that kind of behavior holds zero interest for women who understand men.

Why?

Because when men fight over a woman, it is generally about themselves, not her. As a result, this is rarely if ever the best way for a guy to show that they are worth the

---

30. Not that we are saying anything about Buzzfeed/EOnline/TMZ/*Us* magazine/*Entertainment Weekly*/*New York Post*/Insidr/*The Daily Mail*/ Yahoo!. Not at all. Or about the veracity of what your cousin thought she saw somebody say about the whole fracas on TikTok (maybe). But these things might not always go down *exactly* as reported.

MAKE ROMANCE
COOL AGAIN

As incredible (and incredibly stupid) as this may seem, there are men out there who think it's uncool to be romantic. Best to take a lesson from Pete's book. Yes, even the guy who was sarcastically identified as a "relationship expert" on *Saturday Night Live*'s "Weekend Update" on February 20, 2021, calls himself a "hopeless romantic." He talks about how he tries to "go above and beyond as possible" when he's in a relationship so that the woman he is with can "feel as special as possible." Maybe, just *maybe*, Pete is on to something here with this whole romance thing.

commitment. A good general rule might be for guys to take the energy (time, money, etc.) spent mixing it up with other guys and put it toward a truly romantic gesture for their partner.

Whenever women are polled about things they look for in a man, "throwing down with my annoying ex at the drop of a hat" tends not to crack the top 1,000. (Consider also that a man who's constantly seeking confrontation may not be the most promising dating prospect.)

The guy who can deal with the problem without letting it turn into a fight is easier to be around. Also, the more a man fights with an ex, the more he potentially reminds her that she has an ex she *could* go back to. Why give an ex the spotlight?

When in doubt, stay out of it. Be the lover, not the fighter. And don't text the ex.

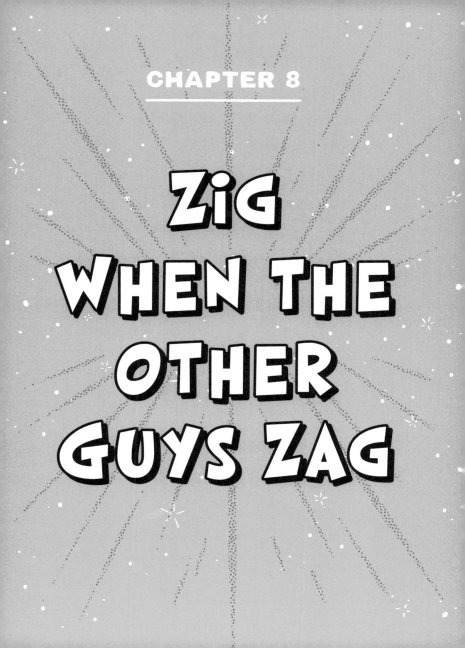

"I GOT ENGAGED [TO ARIANA GRANDE]. NO ONE COULD BELIEVE IT, AND I CAN'T BELIEVE IT. I GET IT. SHE'S THE NUMBER ONE POP STAR IN THE WORLD, AND I'M THE GUY FROM *SNL* THAT EVERYBODY THINKS IS IN DESPERATE NEED OF MORE BLOOD."

—Pete Davidson, "Weekend Update," *Saturday Night Live*, September 29, 2018

id you know that men write for *Cosmopolitan*? It's true. And women write for men's publications like *Maxim* and *Playboy*, the idea being that they can give readers the inside dope on dating and relationships.

A 2014 article in *Cosmopolitan* by Cosmo Frank featured "16 Men Straight Guys Find Attractive." Some of the celebrity dudes who showed up on the list included:

- Ryan Reynolds ("The man is goddamn charming")
- Daniel Craig ("Rough features and rugged charm")
- Channing Tatum ("Funny and nonthreatening")
- Chris Pratt ("The kind of guy I want to eat pizza, drink beer, and play Mario Kart with forever")

Not an especially surprising list for 2014. Or 2024, come to think of it.

More recent versions of that list tend to come up with similar names.[31]

What this list fails to include are men whose appeal other men do not understand. Think of guys like Benedict Cumberbatch, Adam Driver, or Timothée Chalamet. All of them are deemed highly desirable by significant groups of women and some men, but those feelings make little or no sense to large groups of annoyed straight men.[32]

Without getting into a digression on the sexual politics differential between the male and female gaze and how it is reinforced by patriarchal media tropes,[33] suffice it to say that there is usually a world of difference between what women are looking for in a potential boyfriend and what men *think* women are looking for.

Sometimes, certain men's disquiet about the female furor around Pete ends up saying a lot about them.

---

31. George Clooney. Men understand he is attractive. Looks good in a tuxedo. Has his own tequila. Seems like he wouldn't need to be told which fork to use for the appetizer course.

32. *Saturday Night Live* did a sketch on February 1, 2017, with a game show called "Why Is Benedict Cumberbatch Hot?," the premise being that the sketch was written by a jealous and confused male cast member who just didn't get why the women in the show were excited about Cumberbatch being the guest. If Pete had not been in the *SNL* cast at the time, the skit might just as easily have been about him.

33. Though we could totally do that now if you have time. No? *Fine*. Read Laura Mulvey on your own, then.

WHAT MEN **THINK** WOMEN WANT	WHAT WOMEN **REALLY** WANT[34]
Physique	Cute smile, dimples if possible
Money	Steadily employed
Tells killer jokes	Funny (without trying too hard)
Rugged and strong	Gets along with his mother
Constant negging	Thoughtful
Tall	Tall
Symmetrical facial features	That's a thing?

34. Usually. But not always. Really, it changes all the time. Often it is more about the person as a whole than any discrete characteristics you can break down in an oversimplified list like this. Like sometimes it's a turn-on if the guy seems very organized and take-charge and sometimes that can just seem bossy and annoying. Seriously, it's complicated.

For instance: In 2022, rather than passing legislation in order to make things in America just a little bit better than when he came to office, Senator Ted Cruz became quite irate about Pete. Specifically, *Rolling Stone* writer Kat Bouza reported in her May 21, 2022, article "Ted Cruz Just Can't Understand Why All These 'Hot Women' Love Pete Davidson" that the Texas senator bemoaned on his podcast just how much action he thought Pete was getting.

Yes. The *SNL* dude.

This episode raises questions, including why does a sitting senator have a podcast where he talks about who he finds sexy? Also, this was all part of a larger discussion about something Cruz called "toxic femininity," which is particularly confusing.[35]

But perhaps more to the point: Why does Pete just bother some men?

It can't all be attributed to jealousy.

The men who let Pete's dating history get under their skin would be less perturbed by the list of ultra-hot women connected to Tom Brady (*football hero*) or Brad Pitt (*last great American movie star*). Those matchups make sense to the guys annoyed by Pete. For them, men like Brady and Pitt are aspirational figures, with traditionally handsome features and Scrooge McDuck wealth. Men at that level

---

35. What does that mean, anyway? Actually, don't tell us. Better we don't know.

have reached clearly visible targets of wealth and fame. They have also been defined by the mass culture for their looks for long enough that even the average man who does

 **LOVE HiM**

"He seems *genuinely* funny and comparatively normal in a way that is probably refreshing to young women who are on the come-up (or already there) in entertainment and surrounded by a very specific type of Hollywood Straight Guy. There are famous Colin Josts everywhere. Famous Pete Davidsons seem rarer."

—Bobby Finger, jezebel.com, July 14, 2021

"How come that dude gets all of these, like, hot women? Pete Davidson was dating Kate Beckinsale. I mean, you're talking *Underworld*. You're talking super-hot vampire in a black leather trench coat. And you're like, 'Really? The *SNL* dude?'"

—Senator Ted Cruz, on his podcast *Verdict with Ted Cruz*, May 20, 2022

HATE HiM

not read *People* magazine knows Brady and Pitt are in the running for "Sexiest Man Alive."

But discovering that Pete is attractive is something different. If a guy like Pete can be seen as a desirable candidate, some men might feel betrayed. They may have believed that a clearly determined set of goals had been laid out for them and their success with women would to some degree depend on how many of those goals they achieved.

In fact, there is an entire industry dedicated to guys who want these kinds of things laid out for them as clearly as possible. Men can find an entire universe of videos, books, and podcasts dedicated to showing them the cheat codes for how to get women into bed, or just to give them the time of day.[36] According to that school of thought, all men need to do is max themselves out at the gym, act supremely confident and arrogant at all times, flash money and status and luxury purchases, treat niceness and generosity as signs of weakness, and base their entire view of gender dynamics on some very selective readings of evolutionary biology.[37]

36. Of course, there is a quite large media substratum that also provides women with romantic advice. The difference being that it is not all about winning or deception.
37. Don't ask. It's weird.

Then comes Pete:

- ♥ Skinny and string bean–like
- ♥ Dresses at times like a skateboarder who just discovered microdosing
- ♥ Described by many, both appreciators and depreciators, as somewhat "squirrelly"
- ♥ Might lose a fistfight with a twelve-year-old
- ♥ Seems to have money but on an *SNL* and Judd Apatow movie level, not house in the Hamptons or private jet kind of money
- ♥ Funny but also does all that 9/11 material, which is kind of a downer
- ♥ Talks about how crazy and depressed he is

Pete is a problem. He screws up the whole theory.

Looking at all the positive attention getting thrown Pete's way by women, both online and IRL, some guys might wonder: wasn't he the kind of kid who flinched when the jocks walked past him in high school?

They are likely thinking that Pete is no competition.

And yet he is.

Some guys just hate surprises.

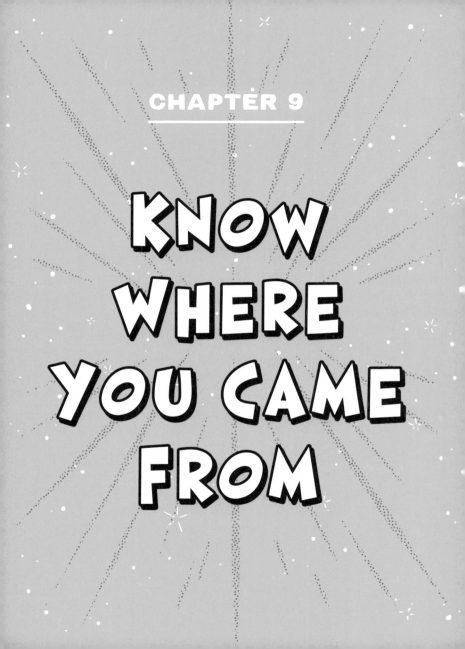

CHAPTER 9

KNOW WHERE YOU CAME FROM

"I'M NO LONGER THE FIRST THING PEOPLE THINK OF WHEN THEY SAY, 'WHAT'S THE WORST THING ABOUT STATEN ISLAND?'"

—Pete Davidson, "Weekend Update," *Saturday Night Live*, December 5, 2020

With most guys, you do not know where they came from. Nor, if we are being truly honest, does anyone really *need* to know.

For some guys, however, the place they were born and raised is very central to their identity. This can be taken in a negative direction.[38] But for the most part, being open about your roots can project a spirit of authenticity and consistency.

If people know anything about Pete, his being a native of Staten Island is probably included. It would almost have to be, given that he has made it a central part of his stand-up act, particularly once he started performing off the island.

Being so up front with his identity gives Pete a few opportunities: It helps create an image right off the bat,

---

38. For example: guys who are just a little *too* much about being from Boston. Enough already. Seriously, stop.

because generally people are going to have a preconception (correct or not) about Staten Island. This might not necessarily be the most positive thing, but it does create a feeling of familiarity. Suddenly, and without much added info, you feel like you already know them.

Pete also plays around with that image. Rather than repeating himself with a few stock lines, or playing uniformly positive or negative, he mixes things up. That turns his history with his birthplace into less of a shtick and something more of an evolving conversation.

So, it's complicated. But complicated is good. Complicated is like an onion, but in a good way. It suggests layers, depth. You know? *Thoughts.*

In some ways, Pete tries to have it both ways.[39] He presents different perspectives on his upbringing and the place that formed him depending on the situation.

There are times when he is the Staten Island salt-of-the-earth guy. Not poor but certainly not from a wealthy background. The kind of guy who would say (as he has) that the only deal breaker for a first date is if the woman is rude to the staff at a restaurant. Firefighter father. Nurse mother. Seeing Manhattan across the water but never getting there until he was a teenager. Believing that, like it or not, that borough was where he was going to spend the rest of his

---

39. Then again, don't we all? And isn't that only fair?

THINGS PETE SAYS ABOUT
STATEN ISLAND

On the One Hand...	*On the Other...*
"It's like a suburb, that's what I like about it."	"It's a terrible borough filled with terrible people."
"I love Staten Island."	"If Staten Island is so desirable, then why is it free to get there?"
"Never forget where you're from."	"[Staten Island guys are like] If you had a Marlboro Red and threw it in the bathtub and it came to life."

life. Possibly the only living man to have a tattoo of the Verrazzano-Narrows Bridge. Performing in local fundraisers. Frustrated that his friends have attitude about the place and make him haul into Manhattan to see them.

There are other times, though, when he is the guy who could not wait to get out of Staten Island. The bullied kid. The one who never felt understood. The one with a chip on his shoulder. Praising the place in an extremely back-handed way ("It's one of those places where you have your few friends and everyone else doesn't like you").[40] Ranting on *SNL*'s "Weekend Update" about COVID regulation pro-testers on Staten Island.

Having it both ways in this manner helps Pete create not just an image for himself but present something of a story. The narrative he crafts is about a guy who grew up in this place that he realizes is part of him, but where he never quite seems to fit in, and potentially where he could land if the whole comedy thing doesn't pan out. It is a backstory rich with detail and drama, complicated in a way that draws us in. The majority of performers like Pete do not seem to exist prior to their first movie, series, or single. Their fame and the current ups and downs of their lives as a famous person are all we care to know about them.

---

40. Not to speak for Staten Island, but it is hard to imagine anywhere wanting to be known as a place that helps people "develop a tough skin."

DOS AND DON'TS OF
DATING UP

DO talk about where you're from.

DON'T act like you're better because of it.

Though not stuck in his past, Pete is continually struggling and in constant dialogue with it. Which is simply far more interesting to any potential paramours than a guy who never self-reflects.

This kind of grounded thoughtfulness also suggests that Pete has the potential to bounce back from future setbacks. He doesn't give off the vibe that he feels entitled to his success, so he's more likely to take obstacles in stride. Guys like Pete who did not have the most fantastic upbringing and did not grow up anywhere glamorous probably have lower expectations about their future.

Everything is a step up.

It could be exciting to go out with a guy like Pete, particularly at the point where his career is really starting to take off. Who wouldn't like that? All the attention, celebrity events, being able to get into any restaurant you want, access to limited-edition sneakers. It could be intoxicating, especially for somebody who hasn't experienced it before.

Yes, Staten Island is easily the most mocked, the most Republican, the most garbage-filled, the most remote, the most commonly forgotten of all New York's boroughs.[41] But it is also in eyesight of Manhattan. Which means something, even if many New Yorkers would publically deny it.

A Staten Islander, even one who basically never goes into the city, is still technically a New Yorker. Almost by dint of living in its shadow, they understand the city to a degree that others wouldn't.

A Kardashian or Grande, accustomed as they are to private planes and private cars and swank urban living, may not seem on the surface to have a lot in common with Pete Davidson, an anxious Staten Islander with Crohn's disease.

But the simple fact that he owns where he is from, and accepts his roots without letting them define him, points to a confidence[42] that a lot of men with something to prove (or hide) would not be able to pull off.

41. Probably something to do with the massive trash dump. And the Mafia. And all the cops. And a lot of things.
42. Remember: This is a guy who told Kim Kardashian not long after they started dating that "I'm gonna grow on you ... give it four months in and you're gonna be obsessed." Oh yes, quite confident.

CHAPTER 10

END ON A HIGH NOTE

"I WILL ALWAYS HAVE
IRREVOCABLE LOVE
FOR HIM."

—Ariana Grande, Instagram, December 3, 2018

Pete definitely does not have a type. Go ahead, find the similarity between Cazzie David and Kate Beckinsale beyond both being women in show business with dark hair. Just try.

When it comes to attracting a new partner, it is best for a man to have some quality relationships in his past. It's like a list of references when applying for a job. That helps validate his experience as a romantic partner.

What gets dangerous (but is also very insightful) is when new love interests start evaluating how he behaved as a relationship ended and after it ended.

Nobody likes a man who cannot manage a clean breakup. The fighting. The back-and-forth. The complaining. The ranting. The lack of showering. Not to mention the excessive hard-seltzer intake.[43] It's unbecoming. Not to mention immature.

---

43. Is there *any* proper amount of hard-seltzer intake? Discuss.

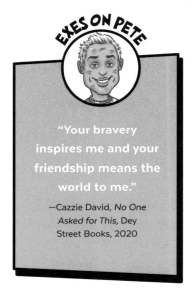

EXES ON PETE

"Your bravery inspires me and your friendship means the world to me."

—Cazzie David, *No One Asked for This*, Dey Street Books, 2020

An inability to conclude a relationship in an orderly manner can disqualify a man from being perceived as prime dating material.

A savvy or, some may say, pragmatic woman knows that no matter how starry-eyed things might be at the start, she and her guy will probably eventually go their separate ways rather than walk down the aisle. Because of that, she might steer clear of a guy who looks like he does not know how to handle a breakup in a calm, cool, and collected fashion. That does not mean she is assuming they will break up. She just does not want to take a risk.

Risky is only sexy when it involves bold romantic gestures, and, depending on the woman, some rebellious forms of transportation.[44] Risky with relationships isn't as enticing. You might think Pete feels risky to women, since he's an actor who is always in the tabloids and has had a lot of girlfriends (and tattoos). But take a moment to look deeper.

---

44. If some women were not attracted to dudes in convertibles, motorcycles, or speedboats, would those things even exist?

WARNING SIGNS
FOR DATING PETE

- ⚠️ Ongoing mental health issues
- ⚠️ Physical ailments
- ⚠️ Serial dater
- ⚠️ Well-documented weed habit
- ⚠️ Poor tattoo-impulse control
- ⚠️ Somewhat lackadaisical approach to work

WELCOME SIGNS
FOR DATING PETE

- 💜 Intensely romantic
- 💜 Has a solid relationship with his mom
- 💜 Goes out but is also okay with Netflix and chilling
- 💜 Seems decent at breaking up
- 💜 Has potential and is open to improvement

DATING UP TIP

Stay classy. Remember that word gets around. People talk. That is all triply true when ending a relationship. All those things you have been meaning to say for months and now think you can because you are broken up? *Do not say them.*

Pete's seeming ability to break up with women in at least outwardly appearing semi-decent fashion is notable.

Mature breakups are not easy to do, especially for celebs. It is pretty easy for a breakup to head south, particularly when there are squadrons of gossip sites ready to shoot the most thinly sourced rumor into the social media stratosphere.

Somehow, Pete seems to have managed it. Even when it would have been easy to create a mess.

Consider when Pete and Cazzie David broke up. The pair was together for about two years. From all indications it was a pretty serious, committed relationship. This despite their different vibes.[45] Things concluded, though, in a spectacularly messy way.

---

45. Him: Class clown-in-training. Her: Type A worrier.

First, David decided she wanted to break up with Pete. They did. She then reconsidered, only to have him tell her he had already moved on.

Bad timing.

David, as she later wrote about in her book *No One Asked for This*, took this poorly. Pete moved right into his next relationship, but he didn't engage in any public fighting. There was some bad blood after the breakup due to his next girlfriend having the kind of fans who felt the need to bully David online. Not great, to put it mildly, but not because of Pete. When asked about their breakup, he calls David a "very talented girl" and says "she'll be great." In other circumstances, this would sound condescending, but considering that she broke up with him and he could be expected to have some negative feelings about that, it could be considered genuine and generous.

His next girlfriend, by the way, was Ariana Grande.

This was a shorter romance, less than six months long, but it was carried out in the full glare of popstar-level fame, with the tensions that come with it.

At this stage, Pete was still getting used to his ugly-hot status and to dating at that level of fame. Prior to that, he was getting photographed largely at events with David and showing up in her social media. With Grande, there were paparazzi staked out in front of her luxury Manhattan apartment ready to get snaps of a couple that the tabloid media could not figure out. Versions of the old "*She's* going out with *him?*" stories proliferated.

Some of Pete's actions during that relationship might have been ill-considered. Like presenting Grande with a $100,000 diamond engagement ring just a few weeks after they first got together. Like getting matching tattoos (see Chapter 11: "Put It in Writing. On Your Body."). Like getting a pet pig together.

But once the Grande relationship was over, he handled himself better than many young men would in the glare of international publicity-hounding. The two broke up in very public fashion but kept it mostly quiet. She kept the pig but gave back the engagement ring. The tattoos they had both gotten about each other were somewhat trickier to manage.

Just a few weeks later, Grande released a song, "thank u, next," with lyrics that explicitly referenced Pete and a video that hinted that she dumped him unexpectedly. She apparently recorded multiple versions of the song, including one where the two *had* gotten married.

As they say, ouch.

Pete mostly kept his thoughts to himself, despite being song and tabloid fodder and despite getting the same Grande-fan bullying that David had. He said nice things about Grande in interviews and called her "a wonderful, strong person." It was well over a year later before he made any jokes at her expense in his comedy, which given his

ANIMAL INSTINCTS

So, the pig thing. Not long after Pete and Grande got together, she decided that she wanted a pet pig. He agreed. Within an hour, as Pete described it on a talk show in 2018, the pig was there. (The power of Grande.) They named the new pet Piggy Smallz, which not only seems unfair to the pig but possibly indicates a couple with poor judgment and (after Pete got a tattoo in the porcine pet's honor) limited impulse control.

habit of unloading about everything in his life is impressive discipline.[46]

Speaking of discipline, even though Pete was quickly attached to a string of new girlfriends in the post-Grande period, those relationships came and went quietly. If the

---

46. Like how after transferring to multiple schools as a kid and being treated terribly at each, he started to realize that maybe *he* was the problem.

breakups were ugly, the public did not know. As far as could be discerned, he stayed on good terms with them all. He apparently left such a good enough impression on

BREAKING UP TIP

Don't end things negatively, especially when you're dating up. Keep it positive, no matter how you feel. Think about Pete's split with Grande. Is it every man's dream to be the subject of an extremely popular song by an ex where she designates him as just another in a series of romances, each of whom provided her with one specific gift before she moved on to the next? No. At the same time, Pete seemed able to keep in mind that it was better to be a guy who has a song written about them than a guy who never inspired a lyric from anyone ever.[47]

---

47. Also, the video shows Grande writing "Pete" in a notebook, under which it reads "I love U always" and "Huuuuuge." Which may have taken even more of the sting away.

Kate Beckinsale that long after they separated, she liked another person's tweet that addressed extreme negative reactions to his dating Kim Kardashian ("everybody refuses to entertain the possibility that he might have a nice personality").

In June 2022, right as a lot of the Davidson-Kardashian media fever was heating up, Pete released a Netflix comedy special titled *The Best Friends*. While the title might give you the idea that it's all about Pete's friends, he actually reveals insights about his

EXES ON PETE

"Pete has got to be literally the best human being I've ever met. People always say, 'He's so funny' ... That's like fourth on my list of why I like him."

—Kim Kardashian, *The Kardashians*, Season 1, Episode 8, June 2, 2022

dating life that outline his "leave on a good note" approach to dating. In the special, Pete handles this by acknowledging the elephant in the room: that West is making overt threats against him. But he subtly undercuts West's power without flexing.

Referencing West's conjecture that Pete had AIDS, Pete says that even though it was absurd, he still went to the doctor because West is a musical "genius," so maybe even the guy who made the song "College Dropout" knows something Pete doesn't. With this joke, Pete manages to take the high road (as a dedicated hip-hop fan, Pete likely really does believe in West's talent) while lightly ridiculing the idea that West knows anything about anything outside of music.

The second noteworthy thing Pete does is include Carly Aquilino in the comic lineup of his special. Even though it had been years since they were (briefly) together, and the relationship did not appear to be that serious, giving her the spotlight was a class move. Particularly given that one of her bits involving her bad taste in men—spotting a guy with multiple facial tattoos at a bar, she thinks "Whatever that is, I will fix it"—could have been taken as an in-good-fun joke at Pete's expense. He also gave Aquilino a role in *The King of Staten Island*.

As far as staying on good terms with your ex goes, that is just about unbeatable.

Follow Pete's example. When potential dates know that you are good at breaking up, that gives them one less reason to avoid you in the first place.

SIX DEGREES OF
DAVIDSON

You've heard of the game Six Degrees of Kevin Bacon. At this point, you could play a version of the game based on the women Pete has dated. Margaret Qualley? Two degrees. (She was in *Once Upon a Time ... in Hollywood* with Brad Pitt, who was in *Sleepers* with Bacon.) Ariana Grande? Three degrees. (She was in *Don't Look Up* with Meryl Streep, who was in *The Laundromat* with Gary Oldman, who was in *JFK* with Bacon.) What does this have to do with Pete's dateability? Well, nothing, really. Except that the more relationships Pete has with people who know a lot of people, then that's more people and romantic prospects for him to meet.

CHAPTER 11

PUT IT IN WRITING. ON YOUR BODY.

"I SAW A PICTURE OF MYSELF WITHOUT A SHIRT. I LOOK LIKE A **TODDLER** WENT TO **PRISON**."

—Pete Davidson, "Weekend Update," *Saturday Night Live*, February 20, 2021

A nybody over a certain age can get a tattoo. That does not mean everybody should get a tattoo. Or lots of tattoos. Or a Pete-level density of tattoos.

But if you are going to get a lot of tattoos, there is an argument for doing it like Pete did.

One study showed that women have more positive reactions to men with tattoos than the non-inked (Galbarczyk and Ziomkiewicz 2017).[48] Many explanations for this have been posed. One study suggested that tattoos were an evolutionary signal from a time when the practice could easily give you an infection. In other words, if a man has

---

48. Not necessarily more *attractive* but healthier and possibly more masculine. In other words, a worthy boost. Everything helps. If you don't want to get a tattoo, you can always work on being attractive in other ways. Like getting a haircut. Or finally washing that shirt. Maybe talking less about mixed martial arts and your no-vegetable diet.

DOS AND DON'TS OF
DATING UP

DO tattoo to express.

DON'T tattoo to impress. Pete's tattoos do not try to present any kind of badass front: no skulls, knives, or the name of his birthplace in gothic lettering. The guy has portraits of Ruth Bader Ginsburg, Hillary Clinton, *and* Willy Wonka on his body. Possibly forever. He is not trying to impress *anybody* with these tattoos. Which is, if you think about it, quite impressive.

visible tattoos and is still walking around upright, you can bet he has a pretty solid immune system.

But nobody ever looked at Pete and thought: Hmm, seems healthy. It is most likely that his tattoos send a different signal. Individuality, perhaps, or the suggestion of a potential mate who is willing to go the extra mile.

An Ipsos.com survey from August 29, 2019, estimated that about a third of Americans were tattooed, with 17 percent having more than one. Among the amply inked, the average number of tattoos was about four. Among the kind of people who spend time online cataloging and parsing the meaning of things celebrities ink on their bodies, the consensus is that Pete has roughly seventy tattoos.

That makes Pete something of a unicorn.

Pete's method of tattooing (selection, placement, execution) is somewhat like his personality and approach to his career: impulsive, unabashedly geeky, limited focus on the big picture, slapdash, and marked by unadulterated honesty.

His tattoos make him an open book. There can be downsides to this, of course. Some women are going to see the word "Warning" tattooed on his wrist or that wolf on his forearm and think, "Naaah. Maybe the guy in the Hilfiger. He looks like he knows the difference between a 401K and a Roth IRA."

But women who see the tattoos and go for it anyway, they have a sense of what they are getting into. They know that they are possibly getting involved with a man who has the phrase "Katy must learn to share with her friends"[49] tattooed on his side. They understand that they are potentially getting into bed with a guy who is a big enough fan of *The Sopranos* to have the logo from the

---

49. No, nobody seems to know what this means. But honestly, isn't it better *not* knowing?

WOMEN:
THEY'RE NOT JUST FOR DATING

While Pete has been romantically linked to many of the women who guest-starred on *Saturday Night Live*, he has still managed to be just friends with some of them. On November 5, 2017, the guest he platonically vibed with was Miley Cyrus. The two performed in a rap video skit in diapers for a song called "Do the Baby Step." So naturally they later got matching tattoos of the phrase "we babies."

This is not to suggest that you run off and get matching tattoos with the next woman you like hanging with. But Pete, who is well-known for throwing himself wholeheartedly into romantic relationships, showed with this that he could also form strong connections with women he was not going out with. Men who have no ability to enjoy nonromantic relationships with women tend not to be the best at communicating with the opposite sex, which can present a serious obstacle when wanting to ask a woman out.

show's strip club Bada Bing! prominently displayed right next to that "Shaolin" tat across his stomach.[50]

To paraphrase what the ever-wise Samuel L. Jackson said about the cinematic classic *Snakes on a Plane*: The title alone tells people whether or not they want to see that movie. Same with Pete's tattoos. They are like a trailer for the attraction that is him.

Pete's seventy-ish tattoos are a guide to not just his likes but his life.

His left arm features a couple of callouts to his father: an especially intricate portrait of a kneeling firefighter as well as his father's badge number. The two mysterious figures on his back—one dark and hooded, the other a winged angel holding a lit cigarette—suggest the dual sides of his nature, the yin and yang pulling him in positive or self-destructive directions.

If Pete has taught us anything about dating up, it's to be raw. Women appreciate men who acknowledge their pain and their emotions as well as their goofiness. Be careful, though. That does not mean every man needs to go out and cover his body in permanent ink that communicates their deepest pain to the world. But it does mean that if you feel the need to open up about something from your past, don't be afraid to do it.

---

50. Almost certainly a reference to Staten Island's martial arts–loving Wu-Tang Clan but possibly also just an indication that Pete likes Buddhist monks who can do kung-fu.

The tattoo map of Pete's body takes us on a journey through all his past relationships.

Getting all those tattoos, and in such rapid succession, presents significant epidermal logistical problems. When you have had numerous relationships in a few years, and feel the need to commemorate many of them on your body, that can add up to a lot of new tattoos. The human body only has so much skin, particularly if you are keeping the face off bounds.[51] Also, new girlfriends may not appreciate seeing so many reminders of his previous loves all over his body. As a result, he has either removed or covered up many of the older tattoos. That giant black keyhole on his side? That's covering up Grande's name.

At the same time, while some women may prefer to never hear or think about the previous loves in their man's life, some might take a different viewpoint. They could see the ink and scars cut across Pete's body and view it as a sign of not only how desired he has been by others (points to her then for snagging him) but also how intense he has been about his relationships. That could bode well for a romantic, if tumultuous, time together.

Most people are not going to follow the Pete route exactly. (Seventy tattoos is a lot of time and a lot of pain.) But the lesson they can take from it is his commitment to

---

51. For now. Never say never.

PETE'S MARKS OF LOVE,
AN INCOMPLETE LIST

CAZZIE DAVID: Her name on his ring finger. A cartoon self-portrait of her, with stars, on his forearm.

ARIANA GRANDE: Small cloud on left middle finger. Trademark rabbit mask behind his left ear. Initials on his right thumb. "Grande" on his side just above the "Bada Bing!" sign. "H2GKMO" on his hand. "*Mille tendresse*" on the back of the neck.[52]

KIM KARDASHIAN: "My girl is a lawyer" on his collarbone. "Aladdin" and "Jasmine," also on his collarbone. "KNSCP" on his neck.[53]

---

52. Grande is into clouds. The acronym stands for "honest to god knock me out." And the phrase is French for "one thousand tendernesses," matching one she has, referencing *Breakfast at Tiffany's*. Grande also seems to be the only one of Pete's girlfriends to get matching versions of several of these herself.
53. Kim was studying for a law degree. Referring to the *SNL Aladdin* skit they starred in together. The acronym is possibly an abbreviation for Kim and the first names of all four of her and Kanye West's children.

"I told Pete, 'Hey, dude, let's just stop with the girlfriend tats' ... Because relationships come and go, and Pete is a really young man. I think that went in one ear and out the other."

—Pete's tattoo guy, Jon Mesa, *New York Post*, June 23, 2018

living his love out loud. His tattoos do not allow much opportunity for hiding the past. This could lead to some awkward pillow talk ("Remind me what 'KNSCP' stands for, again?") but having the words permanently there makes it more difficult to wave the issue away or pretend it never happened. To some degree, it could be helpful to act about your past as though it was already tattooed on your body. No way to ignore it, so you might as well be honest.

Nobody said being a romantic was easy. While many readers might not feel they want to put all that effort (not to mention pain) into having words and designs carved into their skin or lasered off, they may want to consider that what is important about the tattoo is not the thing itself. It is the gesture. And the pain.

For instance, when it was looking like Pete was spending too much time writing out his romances on his body and then erasing them, he made a different gesture. After he started dating Kardashian, he had her name put on his chest. But not as a tattoo. As a brand. As in, a red-hot piece of metal seared "KIM" into his skin.

Say what you will. That is commitment. Yes, they broke up not too long afterward. But at least it's a small brand.[54]

DATING UP TIP

Show that you care. Maybe in your own way. But show it.

It is also inclusive of the other person. While clearly Pete's tattooing (and branding!) habit could be seen as show-offy, he also makes it about the person he is with.

You can have your interests. All men should. (See Chapter 14: "Be Interested, Be Interesting.") Women generally prefer their man to have something going on in his life besides work. It helps take the pressure off them and gives them confidence that you *want* her but don't *need* her to function.

But whatever your thing is, make sure to include her in it. Make it *about* her.

---

54. That act could, though, set a bad precedent. What if he decides later that the brand was not the greatest idea? Then a later girlfriend asks, "So why won't you get a brand with *my* name?" At some point, a line needs to be drawn. Even cows only get branded once.

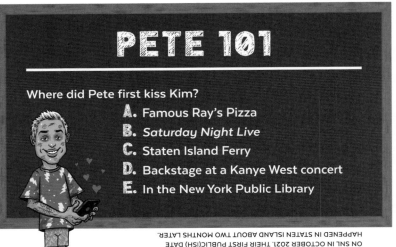

PETE 101

Where did Pete first kiss Kim?

A. Famous Ray's Pizza

B. *Saturday Night Live*

C. Staten Island Ferry

D. Backstage at a Kanye West concert

E. In the New York Public Library

ANSWER: B. THE COUPLE FIRST KISSED WHEN KIM APPEARED ON SNL IN OCTOBER 2021. THEIR FIRST PUBLIC(ISH) DATE HAPPENED IN STATEN ISLAND ABOUT TWO MONTHS LATER.

"THIS IS GOING TO BE A SPECIAL **MOTHER'S DAY** FOR ME BECAUSE THIS YEAR SHE'S NOT JUST MY **MOM**, SHE'S ALSO MY **ROOMMATE**."

—Pete Davidson, "Weekend Update," *Saturday Night Live,* May 11, 2019

Given how much he suffers from anxiety, it's surprising how little Pete cares about what people think. He signals that spirit in many different ways, from his style of dress to his self-mocking jokes to his shrugging "whatever" attitude about the world and its opinions about him.

That attitude is probably nowhere more clearly resonant than in one of the most repeated factoids in nearly any article you read about Pete: He lived with his mom for a while. This by itself is not particularly unusual. Most of us did it for at least the first eighteen or so years of our lives.

But here's the thing: This happened in 2019, when Pete was twenty-six years old. At the time, he was a successful comic. He had been on *Saturday Night Live* for several years and making some bank.[55] That was the year he modeled for Alexander Wang. Things were happening. Things considered quite cool.

---

55. About $15,000 per episode, according to extremely untrustworthy Internet research.

But he still lived with his mother and twenty-one-year-old sister. Which is generally the kind of thing that puts you in the "not cool" category, particularly for somebody who is employed and has options.

Many celebrities, especially those in the hot-up-and-coming category like Pete at that time, would have avoided doing anything like this. Or if they had to, do everything possible to avoid letting the news out. It was understandable why. Pete had plenty of shade thrown his way. One particularly irate woman on Twitter posted that getting "all these chicks while living in your mother's basement" only meant that women didn't know they "deserve better." Even a normally friendly publication like *Vulture* captioned his photo with "Still has BDE (Basement Dweller Energy)" in an April 6, 2021, article.

But rather than ducking for cover, he did what any good comic would do and jiu-jitsu'd the insults by leaning into and twisting them to his advantage.

On "Weekend Update," he argued tongue-in-cheek that living at home made him a "winner." He also reminded people that he wasn't moving back home but had in fact bought the house for his mother (saying that if he buys a place, "I'm going to live in it").

He knew how to handle it. While more insecure men might have denied doing this or refused to talk about it, Pete understood that it was nothing to be ashamed of.

DATING UP TIP

Instead of hiding that one characteristic you fear being judged on (too short? too bald? bad at fashion?), be like Pete and try owning it. Mention it on the first date. Make it sound cool. Be humbled by it. Being upfront and unafraid is an attractive quality, not to mention good sense (people have eyes and word gets out; not mentioning something doesn't make it disappear).

Openly copping to his decision to live with his mother without feeling he had to justify the reasons behind it (whether because he was trying to get sober, get over a breakup, or maybe just spend time with his family) showed confidence and an impressive lack of unnecessary shame.

Like Pete's other out-of-the-box habits, from painting his nails to dating women believed to be far prettier than himself,[56] his basement-living stint might not have made

---

56. Not to mention talking about his Crohn's disease, *a lot*, which is probably listed in some other (lesser, clearly) dating manual as The Thing You Should Never Do.

sense to some people. But it did not seem to hurt his dating chances one bit. Remember, 2019 was just post–Ariana Grande (meaning: Kate Beckinsale, etc.), so his living space was clearly not crimping his dating life.

There are a lot of things people will try to convince you to be embarrassed about. But follow Pete's lead and resist feeling embarrassed about living at home. Too many people online let themselves be shamed by boomers who bought houses in the 1970s for pocket change (or worked their way through college in the years before tuition hit $25,000 a year) and don't get why everybody else can't do the same.

If the women who dated Pete didn't care, then your prospective dates shouldn't, either. Just be prepared to answer some questions.[57]

There are certain things that are different about living at home than having your own place. These range from the good (your mom will *generally* let you slide a few days on the rent; there is usually something in the fridge) to the not-so-good (having your parents wait up for you is no more fun at twenty-six then it was at sixteen).

But either way, living at home means that your parents are around more than they would be otherwise. You can take this as a not-great thing, a doesn't-matter-one-way-or-the-other thing, or a positive thing.

---

57. "Are you planning on getting your own place?" "Is this what your room looked like when you were in high school?" "Do you think they heard us?"

THE SCIENCE OF PETE

In a July 21, 2022, article in *The New York Times*, Anna P. Kambhampaty reported that about a third of Zoomers were living with parents or grandparents and didn't see that changing anytime soon. That's men *and* women, by the way. This is not to say that everybody reading this who is living on their own should immediately post up in their parents' basement. However, if you need to, or already do, there is nothing wrong with that. The same year Pete was living at home, over half of eighteen-to-twenty-nine-year-olds were doing the same.

The positive approach is heartily recommended. That is not just because you (as a normal, functioning human with feelings and a correctly sized non-Grinchian heart) want to maximize the quality time you have in life with your parents.

On top of that, you should also view your parents as a valuable resource. It is generally easier to have a relaxed, friendly relationship with them

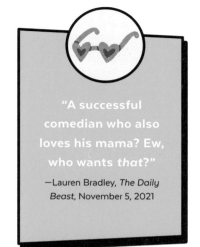

"A successful comedian who also loves his mama? Ew, who wants *that*?"

—Lauren Bradley, *The Daily Beast*, November 5, 2021

as an adult than as an adolescent. Assuming you have done something with your life—maybe not going to law school like your mom wanted since you are so bright, always make such good arguments, and would look just so handsome wearing a suit in a courtroom—then there can simply be less tension and fewer expectations. Establishing a good bond with your parents can then help you when connecting with a girlfriend's parents.

If that is what you want to do.[58]

Some guys who aren't Pete think it's a good idea to be the guy her parents really don't like, the one they warn

---

58. If not, it really should be.

PETE ON PETE

> "I cry a lot. I get into deep conversations. I care about your s---. I like to meet your family. I like to know who you are. And some families are like, 'Who the f--- are you?' So I'm a lot for certain. It was just how I was raised."

—interview with Charlamagne
Tha God, YouTube,
February 24, 2020

her away from. Bad attitude, never on time, sneering at authority, the whole bit. Since you, like all the rest of us, base too much of your life wisdom on things half-remembered from movies and TV shows, you believe that this kind of attitude, guaranteed to make you seem obnoxious to her parents, will make you absolutely irresistible to her. You believe she will crawl across broken glass and ignore a thousand threats from her mother and father to steer clear just so she can breathe your air again.

However, if you would actually like to attract and retain a girlfriend for longer than it took to read that paragraph, do the opposite of that. If you have any aspirations to date up like Pete, you have got to get in good with the parents. What about the rest of the family? you might ask. Do I need to worry what they all think of me as well? The siblings, cousins, and even the weird aunt who works at the prison and always has the worst stories?

Yes, yes, and of course.

What's the best way to do that? There is often not an easy answer. Why? People, a group that includes parents, are weird and unpredictable. Knowing what your girlfriend's parents will like or not like based on nothing more than her saying, "No, they're cool. They'll like you," is a basically impossible task.

At the same time, there are a few solid go-tos that will nearly always turn their favor in your direction.

PRO MOVES
WHEN MEETING FAMILY:

1. Ask to see (or put up with looking at) baby pictures of your date.

2. Insert flattering comments about their beloved child at any possible opportunity.

3. Put effort into making it very clear (whether you do or not) how much it matters that they like you.

Given all that, though, one of the more surefire approaches[59] is to show how nice you are to your own parents.

In the case of Pete, that includes doing everything possible to let the world know that you believe your mother is an absolute saint. People who just barely glean the tabloid news know a few things about Pete, and one of those is that he bought his mom a house worth over a million.

Pete also gives his mom cameo appearances on *Saturday Night Live* and doesn't seem to mind that she hangs out, goes to the after-parties, and makes friends with everybody. Most young men would be worried that their mom would embarrass them. But Pete—whose basement apartment did in fact look like it was designed by a dude who had watched nothing but MTV's *Cribs* his entire life— has the maturity to be comfortable partying with his mom.

A good part of Pete's stand-up material comes from when he was living in his mother's basement. But despite the jokes about her and his sister,[60] and his wondering if it

---

59. Right *after* making sure they see just how intelligent/courageous/unique/ beautiful you believe their daughter to be, and how closely you listen to everything she says.

60. On the May 11, 2019, *Saturday Night Live*, he joked: "It's weird living with my mom and sister because I'll see a strange dude in the house and I don't know if he's some dirtbag preying on my sister or the saint who's going to take my mom off my hands."

was time to go, never for a moment do we doubt his love for his mother and all she put up with.

That capacity for love is something women can see a mile away. They know that the man who is unafraid to gush about his family can also be the one to gush about them. But if you don't express your love out loud, nobody will ever know.

It's like that old rule about writing: Show, don't tell.

"HE PASSED THE CONTENT TAKING **BOYFRIEND TEST**."

—Kim Kardashian, Instagram caption, June 13, 2022

At some point in a new relationship, there comes a time when you have to fit into your girlfriend's life. Sure, you can do all the takeout and *Law & Order* marathons you want. But eventually you have to leave the bedroom. Even Yoko and John finally did.[61] Once that happens, you will inevitably intersect with some aspect of how she spends her time when not romancing you.

This is the Actual Boyfriend stage. Once you have gotten to this point, versions of one or more of the following things might occur:

- ♥ She invites you to this "work drinks thing" at that tiki bar where the little umbrella always goes up your nose when you try and take a sip.
- ♥ Her car is in the shop. She needs a ride to and from work.

---

61. Ask your parents. Or maybe your grandparents.

♥ She has her nephew for the day. He really wants to see the new Marvel movie. She wants you to be there so she can whisper sarcastic dialogue to a grown person.

♥ You arrive at her place just in time to see her mother (who you have not met but recognize from framed pictures) going inside before you.

What do you do in these scenarios? You do what Pete would do. If we know anything about him, it's that he seems to be up for things. Which means a lot coming from a guy like him who has to contend with anxiety and a batch of other mental health challenges. It's a good model to follow. Everyone would rather be with the guy who is up for things than the guy who is like, "Nah, I'm going to chill here."

Actually, this is not even a real question. Because an Actual Boyfriend would *of course* go to the work drinks thing and meet her co-workers, give her all the rides she needs, happily hang out in a movie theater with a six-year-old who demands snacks or a bathroom break every eight-and-a-half minutes, and have coffee in her dining nook while her mother interrogates him about his life choices.

The boyfriend who balks at those things, who tries to weasel out of them and acts as though a relationship can just be two people in a bubble where nothing else matters

DATING UP TIP

Do it. Seriously. Whatever it is. Just do it. Do not complain. Really. It's not going to take that long. What else do you have going on that is so important? Have you any idea what she has done for you? You really don't want to hear the full list of what she's done for you. Because it is long. Come on. Do the thing. It's what successful dating pros like Pete do.

(like her passions, her work, her life) is not really a boyfriend. He is something else.[62]

Through his public dating life, Pete seems to have been the real kind of boyfriend. If not, he has been doing a pretty good job of pretending. Because there he is talking about Cazzie David's dad, going to the MTV Music Awards with Ariana Grande, attending the premiere of Margaret Qualley's movie *Seberg* at the Venice Film Festival, doing the airport pickup with Kim Kardashian.

You know. Boyfriend stuff.

---

62. No, it would not be polite to say what that is.

There are guys who might be okay with doing all those things. It is Venice, after all. It can't always be that big a chore to go out with famous women who have busy professional lives.

But for others, dating Kim might cross the line. After all, she is a different species of celebrity than the others. The others have professions. Singer. Actor. Writer/actor. Kardashian's celebrity business is being herself in all available formats. That is her work. She has over 300 million followers on Instagram.[63] That is not just a business, it is a serious business. And one that a boyfriend will definitely need to be involved in. If he wants to remain the boyfriend.

The phenomenon of the Instagram Husband/ Boyfriend/Whatever has been around almost as long as the app. That would be the significant other who is taking the picture showing his girlfriend/wife as she poses contemplatively on the beach, smiles rapturously with eyes closed while inhaling the scent of a bunch of wildflowers, or does yoga in a minimally decorated loft.[64]

Not long after Pete and Kim became definitely and officially a Thing and some months before they were no

---

63. As of this writing, at least. It might have gone up another half billion by the time you read this. Or Instagram could be over and she and everybody else has ditched it like it was Friendster and moved on to something else. TikTok Now with Smell-o-Vision? Maybe Facebook Classic. Possibly MeowMeowBeenz, who knows?

64. Why, yes, she does have an offer code for those leggings.

longer a Thing, they went on a beach vacation in June 2022. During the trip, Kim put together an Instagram Story filled with pictures of her in a black bikini, usually by herself but occasionally with Pete in the shot, too. When it was just her, though, that was Pete, doing Instagram Boyfriend duty, framing the shot nicely so that his lady looks her best.

They might be on vacation, but she's still working. Pete knows enough to respect that.

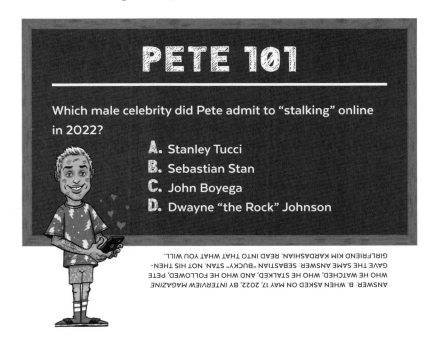

PETE 101

Which male celebrity did Pete admit to "stalking" online in 2022?

A. Stanley Tucci
B. Sebastian Stan
C. John Boyega
D. Dwayne "the Rock" Johnson

ANSWER: B. WHEN ASKED ON MAY 17, 2022, BY *INTERVIEW MAGAZINE* WHO HE WATCHED, WHO HE STALKED, AND WHO HE FOLLOWED, PETE GAVE THE SAME ANSWER: SEBASTIAN "BUCKY" STAN, NOT HIS THEN-GIRLFRIEND KIM KARDASHIAN. READ INTO THAT WHAT YOU WILL.

CHAPTER 14

BE INTERESTED, BE INTERESTING

"KID CUDI SAVED MY LIFE."

—Pete Davidson, interview with *The Breakfast Club*, October 25, 2016

When you first meet somebody where there are romantic possibilities—whether it's shouting over a thudding EDM bass drop at some club, having an awkward first coffee, or having an even more awkward first coffee *after* your first night together—a few things always come up. At some point, one or both of you will talk about what you do when you're not working.

This part of the getting-to-know-you phase can yield a few different responses: a polite but disinterested nod before moving on to something else; a surprised gasp and smiley "same!" reaction; or perhaps a somewhat furtive "get me out of here" look.

Whatever you are interested in, though, no matter what the reaction, it is best to be honest about it. Especially if you are as passionate about anything as Pete is about hip-hop.

When it comes to interests, there are things that we like, things that we love, and things that change our lives.

YOUNG LOVE

Pete loved hip-hop enough that when he was seventeen, he got a tattoo reading "swerve life," referencing a Big Sean song.

For Pete, hip-hop seems to be fully in the "things that change our lives" category. He does not hesitate to drop the names of his favorite rappers at the drop of a hat. Also, he unhesitatingly credits a single hip-hop album, Kid Cudi's moody classic *Man on the Moon,* with giving him the will to go on.

Pete's hip-hop connection goes deeper than that. Though a better comedic actor than he gives himself credit for, he told *Variety* magazine in an August 28, 2018, interview that his inability to avoid cracking up in skits on *Saturday Night Live* was because he sucks at acting. "I'm not a good actor," he proclaimed, "Like, you hired me, it's not my fault."[65] That might be somewhat true; he does seem most himself when just riffing to the audience on "Weekend Update."

---

65. Assuming he would be fired at any moment turned out to be one of Pete's most potent superpowers. He took weeks off from *SNL* to do other projects since he believed he was about to be canned anyway, didn't complain about acting in relatively few skits, and mocked his own acting abilities. And yet remained a star.

With one exception: the hip-hop videos he made for *SNL*. From a realistically annoying SoundCloud rapper to solid impersonations of Lil Pump and Eminem, to duets with heavy hitters like Megan Thee Stallion, Method Man, and Bad Bunny, Pete manages to go well beyond fanboying in the videos he produced. His passion for the music and the culture is clear—and that's what makes it compelling. He embodies the outsized swagger of these characters in a way that he rarely could in his other, largely autobiographical work. In one video, playing a blinged-out MC version of himself in a duet with Taylor Swift, arguably the largest pop star in America at the time, he more than held his own in the glare of her fabulosity.[66] He delivers the same depth of credibility to other videos, making it clear that this fascination is organic and far from performative.

Pete's love of hip-hop seems to come from such a deep place that it allows him to step outside himself. That love comes through in a genuine enough fashion that watching him play those characters can generate joy even in people with no love of the genre itself.

Pete also eagerly shares other enthusiasms, whether it's his love for Harry Potter, movies, other branches of pop music (unless he is just faking it to make his friend Machine

---

66. Some of her fans might have been wondering (hoping? worrying?) that they would soon be reading cryptic social media from Taylor that suggested something was happening between the two.

Gun Kelly feel better during his pop-punk phase), and of course, tattoos.

Whatever interests you have in your life, if there is one that you feel bonded with to that degree, share it. Avoid looking like a guy who might only love himself.

If Pete is any example, sharing your interests with the world will make you attractive in a way that no one, maybe even you, ever suspected.

"I WAS A **HUGE** HARRY POTTER FAN WHEN I WAS A KID TWO YEARS AGO."

—Pete Davidson, "Weekend Update," *Saturday Night Live*, May 16, 2015

Part of Pete's mysterious capacity to attract hotties lies in his boyish approach to everything. His inner child is also his outer child, with no pretense of acting like a regular, boring adult. His dates know they'll have a front row seat to the wide-eyed adventure and highs and lows of his life experience. They want the romance, of course. But fun is attractive, too.

Like pretty much every other millennial, Pete grew up with the Harry Potter franchise. You could say that the world of the boy wizard was to millennials what *Star Wars* was to Gen X, but the Gen Xers grew up with only three movies from that franchise.[67] Fans of J. K. Rowling's magic world had eight, not to mention the novels, theme parks, and everything else.

---

67. Unless you count the *Star Wars Holiday Special*. Bea Arthur runs the Mos Eisley cantina. Jefferson Starship performs via hologram. Chewbacca's family is there. Seems like it deserves inclusion.

Because Pete was even more of a fan than the average millennial, he expressed that admiration the best way he knew how: by getting a tattoo. At last sighting, the uplifting quote from Dumbledore—"Happiness can be found, even in the darkest of times, if one only remembers to turn on the light"—can be seen on his inside left forearm.

So far, so nerdy. But while plenty of millennials would be fine copping to their Potter fandom and sporting a Potter-themed tattoo from when they were younger, some might be uncomfortable geeking out the way Pete ended up doing.

In 2018, Pete and Ariana Grande made their relationship Instagram official by posing for a picture in robes depicting which of the Potter series' four houses of wizards they imagined they would belong to. It's a charming move, not to mention a revealing one. She's Slytherin. He's Gryffindor.

Even though the true depth of Pete's Potter fandom was dissected and criticized online at various points,[68] his choice of wizarding house seems on-point:

Hufflepuff? Too diligent and stable.
Ravenclaw? Too organized.
Slytherin? Way too ambitious.[69]

---

68. Because of course it was.
69. Keen organizational skills and a penchant for evil aren't really Pete's brand. Nor should they be yours.

The standard take on Gryffindors is that they're the heroes: brave, stand-up people who role-model chivalry and are always helping their friends out. According to the Wizarding World website, even though Gryffindors often get stereotyped as attention-seekers showing off their courage to the world, that does not mean they are all sub-limely self-assured. Gryffindors can be anxious and shy and ambivalent about the spotlight, without a tendency to boast. That is not to say Pete is any Neville Longbottom,[70] but Pete's courage—holding his ground without trying to start fights, admitting freely to his issues, never showing false bravado—is no less visible for being quiet.

Pete shows us that you can reveal your personality to people without coming out and saying what you are like or making them wait around for months to see how you respond in different situations. Putting on a wizarding robe can be a decent shortcut. Indulging your inner child and flaunting your fascination with fictional characters is, surprisingly enough, sexy.

Especially if you're a Gryffindor.

Find your shortcut. Don't worry about how attractive or charming you think you aren't and just act as if you are. Pete proves to the world that anyone has a shot at unbridled

---

70. Shy kid? Didn't quite fit in at Hogwarts? No? Well, read the books again. You'll see.

success. Show the A-listers in your life your inner hotness and you, too, can date up.

But what does this all mean? you might be asking. *What does it have to do with me?* you might also be asking. That's understandable. You, dear reader, might not be a scrawny, quirky, elaborately and frequently poorly tattooed comedian from Staten Island. That's okay. Nearly none of us are.

That doesn't mean you don't have anything to learn from Pete. Not that everyone needs to follow what he did. After all, the number of people in this world who can get laughs on a comedy club stage from telling jokes about their Crohn's disease is probably pretty minimal.

But what Pete's shining example can teach every single person reading this book is this: Care about the things that matter and forget the rest.

Be undefinable. Be surprising. Be up for anything. Be spontaneous, weird, kind, loving, and maybe a little too honest about yourself. Hold nothing back.

And you never know what kind of love or attention you might attract. Anything is possible.

Pete clearly never thought he was hot.

The world, and some of its hottest inhabitants, beg to disagree.

REFERENCES

Ainsworth, Sarah E., and Jon K. Maner. Sex Begets Violence: Mating Motives, Social Dominance, and Physical Aggression in Men. *Journal of Personality and Social Psychology* 103.5 (2012): 819-29. https://www.goodtherapy.org/blog/men-fight-violence-women-dominance-control-1128123.

Allie, Jones. "The Adventures of Pete Davidson." *GQ*, August 16, 2018. https://www.gq.com/story/pete-davidson-style-2018.

Arnold, Amanda. "Pete Opens Up about Dating with Borderline Personality Disorder." *The Cut*, May 24, 2018. https://www.thecut.com/2018/05/pete-davidson-dating-mental-illness-borderline-personality-disorder.html.

Ben-Zeév, Aaron, Ph.D. (2021). "So, you want to impress her? Make her laugh." Psychology Today.

Bouza, Kate. "Ted Cruz Just Can't Understand Why All These 'Hot Women' Love Pete Davidson." *Rolling Stone*, May 21, 2022. https://www.rollingstone.com/politics/politics-news/ted-cruz-pete-davidson-podcast-comments-1356755/.

Bradley, Laura. "Please Stop Pretending That Pete Davidson Isn't Hot." *The Daily Beast*, November 5, 2021. https://www.thedailybeast.com/please-stop-pretending-that-pete-davidson-isnt-hot.

David, Cazzie. *No One Asked for This*. New York: Dey Street, 2020.

Durham University. "Men fighting over women? It's nothing new, suggests research." ScienceDaily. www.sciencedaily.com/releases/2008/06/080602214132.htm (accessed January 2, 2023).

Frank, Cosmo. "16 Men Straight Guys Find Attractive." *Cosmopolitan*, September 24, 2014. https://www.cosmopolitan.com/entertainment/celebs/news/g4339/straight-man-ranks-hottest-guys/.

Galbarczyk, Andre, and Anna Ziomkiewicz, "Tattooed men: Healthy bad boys and good-looking competitors." Personality and Individual Differences 106, 122-125 (2017).

Geher, G., and S. B. Kaufman (2013). Mating intelligence unleashed. Oxford University Press.

Grossman, Lena. "Pete Davidson Jokes about Rehab and Being 'So Lame' in High School." *E! News*, January 28, 2019. https://www.eonline.com/news/1009293/pete-davidson-jokes-about-rehab-and-being-so-lame-in-high-school.

The King of Staten Island (2020).

Kupfer, Lindsey. "Pete Davidson Tried to Get Kim Kardashian's Number from Megan Fox before 'SNL.'" *New York Post*, June 2, 2022. https://pagesix.com/2022/06/02/pete-davidson-tried-to-get-kim-kardashians-number-before-snl/.

Nicholson, Christine. "The Humor Gap." *Scientific American*, October 1, 2012. https://www.scientificamerican.com/article/the-humor-gap-2012-10-23/.

Pete Davidson: Alive from New York (2021).

Pete Davidson: SMD (2016).

Pete Davidson Presents: The Best Friends (2022).

Rizzo, Laura. "How Did Pete Davidson Get Famous?" *Life & Style*, November 11, 2019. https://www.lifeandstylemag.com/posts/how-did-pete-davidson-get-famous-stand-up-comedy-mtv-and-snl/.

Rosenberg, Rebecca. "Accused Pete Davidson Stalker Allegedly Barraged Him with Unwanted Gifts." *New York Post*, March 19, 2021. https://pagesix.com/2021/03/19/accused-pete-davidson-stalker-allegedly-barraged-him-with-unwanted-gifts/.

Sanchez, Rosa. "Kim Kardashian Holds Pete Davidson's Hand at the Met Gala in Marilyn Monroe's Vintage Dress." *Harpers Bazaar*, May 2, 2022. https://www.harpersbazaar.com/celebrity/latest/a39828655/kim-kardashian-pete-davidson-marilyn-monroe-dress-met-gala-2022/.

Saturday Night Live, NBC.

Street, S. E. et al. Human mate-choice copying is domain-general social learning. Scientific Reports 8, 1715 (2018).

Vakirtzis, Antonios, and S. Roberts "Nonindependent mate choice in monogamy." Behavioral Ecology 21, 898-901 (2010).

Zinoman, Jason. "Pete Davidson's New Special Seems Like It Needs a Hug." *New York Times*, February 26, 2020. https://www.nytimes.com/2020/02/26/arts/television/pete-davidson-whitmer-thomas.html.